How
to Be
a Budget
Fashionista

How to Be a Budget Fashionista®

The Ultimate Guide to Looking Fabulous for Less

Kathryn Finney
Founder of TheBudgetFashionista.com

Ballantine Books 🏙 New York

A Ballantine Books Trade Paperback Original

Copyright © 2006 by Kathryn Finney

All rights reserved.

Published in the United States by Ballantine Books,
an imprint of The Random House Publishing Group,
a division of Random House, Inc., New York.

BALLANTINE and colophon are registered
trademarks of Random House, Inc.

BUDGET FASHIONISTA is a registered trademark
of Kathryn Finney.

ISBN 0-8129-7516-2

Printed in the United States of America

www.ballantinebooks.com

987654321

Book design by Mercedes Everett

Illustrations by Aimee Sicuro and
Tobias Wright

Contents

What's a Budget Fashionista?

budget: a systematic plan for the expenditure of a usually fixed resource, such as money, during a given period.

fashionista: an ardent follower of fashion and the fashion industry. —*The New Webster Dictionary*

budget fashionista: someone who effortlessly combines personal style with financial savvy. —*The Budget Fashionista*

Welcome to the ultimate guide for those who, whether by choice or by limited funds, want to look fabulous for less. Let's be honest: We're living in cash-poor but image-conscious times. Luxury retailers such as Saks Fifth Avenue compete for profits and retail space with off-price retailers like H&M. Canal Street, New York City's home of the designer knockoff, receives as many tourists as Fifth Avenue. Kim Cattrall, whose *Sex and the City* character Samantha Jones became the poster child for postmenopausal sexuality, has fueled the once dormant inner fashionista of thousands of budget-conscious baby boomers. Everyone wants designer clothes. And they want them cheap.

In three easy steps you'll learn budget secrets like how to score great finds from designers such as Prada and Kate Spade for more than 75 percent off, instructions for how to put together a sizzling work wardrobe for under $200, tips on raising dough for seasonal shopping sprees, and lessons on how to work the Internet to find unbelievable deals. In addition, I'll share tips on how to mix Mossimo with Missoni and Etro with J. Lo, the key to spotting a fake Louis Vuitton bag, how to spot trends before they happen, tips on creating irresistible outfits from discount stores like T.J. Maxx, and a road map to crafting your own delicious style.

I'm not rich. I'm not a size 2. I'm not even from New York. I'm just a brilliantly normal person who was lured into the evils of credit card debt by an obsession with handbags and designer shoes. For example, once I bought eleven pairs of shoes from the clearance rack at a local DSW. Another time I spent ten hours on eBay searching for a genuine Chloe Paddington bag for less than $250 (doesn't exist).

In a six-year period I forgot all my Midwestern frugalness and racked up over $20,000 in credit card debt and a whole mess of student loans. There's a strong likelihood that my firstborn child will be named Visa. Walking the edge of bankruptcy (and marrying someone cheap) helped me change my dangerous shopping ways and get out of debt the old-fashioned way: one payment at a time. But I loved fashion, especially shoes. I knew there had to be a way to be fiscally responsible and stylish at the same time. Like a Chanel-clad phoenix rising from the ashes of financial stupidity, this book emerged.

As The Budget Fashionista I'm the patron saint of budget shopping. To the thousands of readers of my site, TheBudgetFashionista .com, and readers of my syndicated column in magazines like *Budget Savvy Living,* I'm known as the go-to person for guidance on how to look fabulous for less. I'm fearless in my pursuit of the sale, defying the laws of shopping gravity by jumping over sale racks in a single bound. Credit card companies fear me, friends call me for advice, and my bank loves me. I dumped my complete bag of money-saving fashion tips into this book in order to help you become a true budget fashion shopper.

Timeline of The Budget Fashionista

1976   Fashionably late for birth.

1980   Gave first fashion-related lectures at the Teaching Center Preschool in Milwaukee, Wisconsin. Featured topics were the importance of color coordination and the thrill of Buster Brown shoes.

1982   Designed a complete back-to-school look for Barbie and a cheaper bridge line for Skipper.

1983   Began an obsession with undergarments after receiving a pair of Wonder Woman Underoos.

1985   Convinced older brother to throw away his brown corduroy pants because when he walked, the swooshing sound of the corduroy "gave me a headache."

1988   Used money and connections obtained through a lucrative friendship bracelet business to purchase a cloth Esprit bag for an extra 25 percent off.

1990   Obtained first personal styling client, friend Annie. Designed and created outfits for my fellow classmates at Susan B. Anthony Junior High.

1992   First job: peon at a clothing store in the Mall of America, the largest mall in the United States.

1993   Invoking the spirits of divas past, wore Jackie O. sunglasses throughout prom night. (Can't describe prom date.)

1994   Skipped freshman orientation at college to attend first sample sale.

1995   Wrote first fashion article, titled "The Seven Evils of Wool."

1996   While living abroad, learned how to say "cheap" in four languages.

1998   Became skilled in the "art of Ikea" while decorating first apartment.

2001   Began paying student loans, spurring the creation of The Budget Fashionista.

2002   Attended first New York City Fashion Week. Have yet to recover.

2003   Launched the Budget Fashionista website.

What Is a Budget Fashionista?

A budget fashionista is a fearless shopper, one who is so fabulous that her style extends past economic constraints. Unlike general "fashionistas," we aren't slaves to trends. In fact, budget fashionistas pride themselves on their ability to forecast trends and save money by being ahead of the curve. We have great style and a solid 401(k). We pay more attention to what flatters our natural beauty than to the latest fad because we know that a designer label is less important than looking fabulous. We started shopping at Target when Isaac Mizrahi was still in design school, and we can create incredible outfits from a trip to the local Wal-Mart. We can tell you when Macy's has its annual sales (it is posted on a calendar in our PDAs), and our numbers are on speed dial at the local Salvation Army, where we spend as much as we donate. Some of us are budget fashionistas by choice and some by necessity, but we're all fabulous.

Budget Fashionista Tip #1: Buy What You Love and Love What You Buy

Repeat this tip to yourself before you enter a store, while trying on clothes in the dressing room, and while waiting at the cash register at your favorite store. Feel empowered to say no to useless trends, stand-alone pieces, and overpriced designer items that make you look anything but your absolute best. Approach shopping like you would approach a marriage. Would you marry a person you just "liked"?

Being a budget fashionista doesn't mean staying away from the mall or putting online shopping sites on parental lock. Budget fashionistas still buy clothes—but the right clothes that leave them with a great closet and great bank account. You can have both. Don't forget to pay close attention to each step because after reading this book, you will have the chance to test your savvy shopping skills online at TheBudgetFashionista.com and become a Certified Budget Fashionista.

So gather your bank statements, grab a tote bag, put on your shopping sneakers, and let's begin.

Stylish Spendthrifts vs. Fabulously Frugal: The Difference Between a Fashionista and a Budget Fashionista

Fashionista	Budget Fashionista
Fashion determines personal style	Personal style complements fashion
Has a paid subscription to *Vogue*	Reads Style.com (*Vogue*'s website) for free
Has a closet full of pointy shoes and massive podiatrist bills	Has stock in Dr. Scholl's
Can refer you to her accountant	Can tell you the amount of her last purchase
Shops at Neiman Marcus	Shops at Last Call Neiman Marcus outlet store
Uses her kids as an accessory	Accessorizes her kids
Has massive credit card debt	Knows her FICO score and the FICO score of her five closest friends

Step 1

Know Your Budget

*L*ike the whooping crane and great-fitting jeans, budgeting is now extinct. The rise of credit and debit cards has made items that our foreshopping mothers had to wait months to purchase as accessible as whipping out our plastic friends—a major reason so many fashionistas like myself are in debt. Managing your money, including credit, is as big a part of being a budget fashionista as bargain shopping at the local discount store.

Somehow we've lost the art of shopping anticipation. Gone are the days of layaway, when stores allowed you to "hold" items for months, paying set amounts in cash until the purchase was paid in full. Even if you are a stellar budgeter, you've probably fallen prey to "buy-it-now-ism." Take a moment and think about the last time you actually saved up for something. If you can remember that far back, remember the sense of pride and accomplishment when you saved enough to purchase the item. The immediate reward for saving was the satisfaction of knowing that the item you purchased was completely yours. The ultimate reward was better credit.

| A Budget Fashionista Dilemma: What We Want vs. What We Can Afford ||
What We Want	What We Can Afford
Hermès Birkin bag	Classic Coach bag
Roberto Cavalli dress	Rampage dress
Chanel suit	DKNY suit
Manolo Blahnik sexy heels	Unlisted sexy heels
Burberry trench coat	Anne Klein trench coat

Looking fabulous and reducing debt are not mutually exclusive. In this step I'll show you how to do both at the same time. All it takes is a little multitasking and some discipline. Even if you're someone who looks forward to balancing your checkbook, you'll learn innovative ways to track, save, and earn more dough, like the Saver's Rule and hosting a clothing swap party.

In the first chapter you'll learn how to develop your budget skills and ways to infuse much needed dollars into your monthly budget. By resurrecting the lost art of shopping anticipation, having a clear picture of your financial situation, and realizing that a pair of Manolo Blahnik strappy heels does not constitute an investment in your retirement fund, you will have not only a more secure future but also more money for shopping.

If you're like me, you're probably tempted to skip this step and head on over to "Step 2: Know Your Style" (page 37). Many of us dread creating a budget as much as we dread going to the gynecologist. I mean, who really *wants* to be on a budget? However, the thing you dread most (creating a budget) is exactly what is going to help you be fabulous for less. Read this section and find out how.

Chapter 1

Budgeting 101

Raise your hand if you have ever experienced consumer cramps. This is not to be confused with the "other" cramps. Consumer cramps, a.k.a. buyer's remorse, is the feeling you get in the pit of your stomach when you purchase an item that you know will wreak havoc on your finances. Consumer cramps come when you spend, say, $800 on a designer bag and realize that you now have barely enough money for the rent. In my case, buyer's remorse is spurred on by the excitement of a sale. Like the time I purchased a beautiful black cardigan at Macy's one-day sale, got home, and realized that I already had two similar beautiful black cardigans in my closet.

Budget Fashionista Tip #2: Keep the Receipts

Save all tags and receipts for at least two weeks after you purchase an item. Go to your local Office Max or Staples and purchase a coupon or bill folder. Number each tab in the folder according to the days of the month and place your receipts in the folder at least three days before the last day to exchange or return the item.

Learning how to spend and save wisely is the Advil for consumer cramps; you will enjoy a lifetime of relief. In this chapter you'll learn how to create a budget that is both savings and shopping friendly. At its end you will feel empowered to make the financial changes necessary for becoming a budget fashionista!

Telling a fashionista not to spend money on designer clothes is like telling the sun not to rise. It's just not going to happen. Fashionistas love to look great, and, unfortunately, that does cost some money. However, the most important element to looking great is style—something you can't buy. No matter how many Manolos you have stuffed in your closet, you won't look good if you can't afford a pedicure to remove the crusty dead skin from your heels. Having a Louis Vuitton bag won't increase your style quotient if you're so broke that you can't afford a studio apartment on skid row.

The Budget Fashionista Explains: Why You Should Start a Budget

Budget fashionistas know how to manage their checkbook and their closets. They know that sometimes they might need a little extra help, such as when I sought the help of a financial adviser to help me manage my financial assets. She helped me realize that the $50 U.S. Savings Bond my grandpa gave me when I was twelve didn't constitute an established savings plan.

Thank God for financial planners like Janine Moore. This financial diva, a founder and a principal in Peak Financial Group, LLC, understands the lure of a good sale and the constraints of debt. While attending Ohio State University, she rang up over $5,000 in credit card debt shopping at JC Penney. Developing a budget helped her rein in her expenses and get rid of debt. Janine offered these five reasons fashionistas should develop a budget:

Reason #5: Buying a house is impossible if your credit is jacked.
Reason #4: Dodging creditors' calls is no fun.
Reason #3: Saving a *little now* beats saving *a lot* later.
Reason #2: Having plastic surgery done on your credit cards is less painful than having it done on your body.
Reason #1: Having *more money to spend* on yourself is feasible if you don't have any debt!

True Shopping Confessions:
Real Shopping Budgets from Real Women

According to my Annual Shopping Survey, women spend approximately $316 per month on personal clothing, including accessories. (I spend approximately $200 per month on personal clothing.) Here are the monthly shopping budgets of some of the survey respondents:

Cory, a twenty-year-old college student from Long Island, spends $1,000 (yep, a thousand bucks) per month on clothing.

Melanie, a twenty-three-year-old administrative assistant who lives in New York City, spends $50 per month on clothing.

Sandra, a twenty-eight-year-old law student in Chicago, spends about $300 per month on clothing.

Colette, a twenty-nine-year-old married mother of one with a new mortgage and a new baby in Los Angeles, spends approximately $200 per month on clothing.

Kate, a thirty-nine-year-old fashion editor in New York City, spends approximately $400 per month on clothing.

Earline, a fifty-five-year-old tech consultant and divorced mother and grandmother in North Carolina, spends on average around $100 a month on clothing.

Karen, a fifty-eight-year-old widow in Minnesota, spends $200 to $300 per month on clothing.

During the summer of 2005 I conducted a somewhat scientific survey of the over fifteen thousand active recipients of The Budget Fashionista newsletters in an effort to find out what is "normal" in regard to shopping, budgets, and purchases. More than eight hundred fashionistas responded to the anonymous survey, and their true shopping confessions are placed throughout the book. What I found out was that when it comes to shopping, one size doesn't fit all. Respondents' shopping budgets ranged from a paltry $25 per month to an excessive $3,000 a month. What you spend per month on clothing is, and should be, a function of your job, your geographical location, and your personal finances. The Saver's Rule can help you figure out how much you should be spending per month on shopping.

Budget Fashionista Tip #3: The Saver's Rule

Here is a little-known fact: The more you save, the more and longer you will be able to spend. Budget fashionistas must save at least as much as they spend on clothes per month. For example, if you have $250 after paying all your expenses, at least $125 of it should go into your savings account. Deposit the other $125 into a completely separate interest-bearing checking or savings account with its own debit card and checks, to be used specifically for shopping. That way you will be able to keep track of the money you spend on clothes.

Opening an interest-bearing savings account for your shopping funds is quite easy. If you have an existing relationship with a bank, ask one of the personal bankers if the bank has shopping savings accounts. These are special accounts that sometimes have slightly higher interest rates than a traditional account, allowing shoppers to save toward big purchases. If your bank doesn't have them, just open a regular savings or checking account dedicated solely to your shopping purchases.

Cutting Back

You have two basic choices to improve your budget: You can either increase your income or decrease your spending. I suggest doing both. In Chapter 2 I'll show you ten ways to infuse cash into your bank account. I've used several of these methods to put dollars into my bank account. Dough-raising methods 3 and 4 (selling items to consignment stores and selling on eBay; see pages 23–27) were particularly effective in infusing much-needed cash into my budget. However, the easiest way to tilt the budget scale toward positive is to cut back on your expenditures.

Cut Back	Budget Benefit (per Year)	Life Benefit	What It Could Buy
Cable	$360 plus	Increased intelligence	A pair of Christian Louboutin sandals at Last Call Neiman Marcus sale
Specialty coffee	$1,560	Weight loss	A real Louis Vuitton baguette from eLuxury.com
Eating lunch out	$1,860	Salary raise	A Max Mara winter coat from Saks Fifth Avenue, a matching hat and glove set from Target, and a Coach tote bag
Eating dinner out	$1,875	Culinary skills	A Chanel suit at a high-end con-signment shop and a pair of Jimmy Choos from Barneys New York

The table above demonstrates how cutting back on simple items like trips to the local Starbucks and purchasing lunch every day can save you tons of money—enough to help fund a new wardrobe.

Building Your Own Budget

In any good relationship both partners must be committed to building and growing the relationship. In order to build a committed, loving relationship with your finances, you must first investigate your own feeling toward money. Suze Orman, the financial guru, states in her book *Financial Guidebook: Put the 9 Steps to Work,* "Financial freedom begins not in a bank or even in a financial planner's office, but in your mind. It begins with your thoughts." Right on, Suze. So put your thinking caps on and ask yourself the following questions:

• Do I forget to balance my checkbook and rarely review my monthly statements?

- Do I spend more on clothes and accessories than I do on a savings plan?
- If I lost my job today, would I be unable to pay my essential bills?
- Do I consistently use credit cards to purchase basic items like groceries?

If you answered yes to any of these questions, then developing a budget is crucial to help you create a savings plan that is shopping friendly. Developing a relationship with an accountant can help you to manage your finances. You may also want to contact a certified financial planner (CFP). CFPs are financial professionals who have taken additional courses and passed a ten-hour examination on advanced personal finance–related topics such as life insurance, securities, and taxes. Although they charge a fee, CFPs can help fashionistas who need that extra push to make the budget cuts necessary to become a budget fashionista. To learn more about CFPs, visit the Certified Financial Planners Board of Standards, Inc. (www.cfp.net).

Steps to Building a Budget

1. Print out or ask your bank for your statements from the last three months. Gross salary is great, but you need to know exactly how much is put into your bank account after taxes (net earnings).
2. Gather all credit card bills from the past three months, organizing them in order of high to low interest rate.
3. When developing your budget, make sure to include all credit card purchases. Credit card money is *real* money.

Make creating your budget an event! Play your favorite CDs. If you love rock and roll, put on some Rolling Stones and roll right through your budget planning. If you like R&B, put on Destiny's Child and get organized to pay your bills. Jazz lovers, let Coltrane help you speed your way through your financial planning. Once you have the music, make yourself a little

YOUR BUDGET FORM

Item	Amount Per Month	Comments
INCOME		
Your salary		
Your spouse's/ partner's salary		Include other forms of income from gigs, property, etc.
Other income		
TOTAL INCOME		
EXPENDITURES		
Basics		
Rent		
Utilities		
Groceries		
Child care		
Car and property insurance		
Health insurance, prescriptions, etc.		A tube of MAC lipstick doesn't qualify.
Gasoline		
Telephone		
Internet		
Total Basics		
Loans/Debts		
Credit card debt		Always try to send a little extra each month.
Student loans		
Car loan		

Mortgages		
Personal loans		Pay back loans from family and friends.
Other loans and debts		
Total Loans/Debts		
Extra Stuff		You really don't *need* any of this stuff, but it sure makes life sweeter.
Cell phone		
Cable/satellite		
Entertainment		
Dry cleaning		
Subscriptions		
Clothing/accessories Personal		
Clothing/accessories Others		Clothing for spouse/ partner, children, boyfriend, dog, etc.
Other expenditure		
Other expenditure		
Other expenditure		
Total Extra Stuff		
TOTAL EXPENDITURES		

My Total Income: _____

My Total Expenditures: _____

Total Amount Left Over: _____

Hopefully you have a positive figure for the Total Amount Left Over line above. If you do, take half of the amount and place it in an interest-bearing shopping savings account. Take the other half and put it in other savings or investment options such as mutual funds or a money market account. If you don't have a positive figure for the Total Amount Left Over Line, take some time to review your budget and mark places where you can cut back.

cocktail. There's nothing like a cocktail to help you get through any financial-based depression.

Tracking your budget is much easier if you use a spreadsheet program like Microsoft Excel or a personal financial program like Quicken or QuickBooks. You can purchase a version of the software at any Best Buy or Circuit City store, or you can buy online at eBay.com and save a few bucks (make sure it is a legal copy). Either way, these programs make it easier to manage all your accounts in one place. This is important because it allows you to see what kind of a dent you are making, if any, in your debt. Also, it allows you to link your budget to your bank account.

The Budget Fashionista Explains: How to Save When You Really Want to Spend

One of the hardest lessons for a fashionista transitioning into a budget fashionista to learn is how to save when you really want to spend. After a few years of marriage, my husband and I decided to build a little equity by purchasing our first house, which meant we were operating on a strict budget, something that wasn't exactly my strong suit at the time. What should have been a pretty easy task turned into a battle of epic proportions: Equity vs. Armani. Tax breaks vs. Lenox plates. A 20 percent down payment vs. 20 percent off at Bloomingdale's.

Whether you're saving for a house, a new car, or a much-needed vacation, the tips below will help you curb your spending and increase your savings:

1. **Place an address label over debit and credit cards with statements to remind you of your goal.** Try statements like "What would Suze Orman do?" "Equity is love," "Closet vs. house," or my personal favorite, "You ain't Oprah." Every time you reach into your wallet to use the card, your saying will remind you not to spend.
2. **Launder your money.** At the beginning of each week take out all your spending

money—I mean everything in cash (including grocery money)—and hide your wallet in your dirty clothes hamper. When it's time to do your weekly laundry, it's time to take out more spending money.

3. **Window-shop from a distance.** Drive to a mall that is very far from your home to go shopping and bring only $10 in cash with you.

4. **Shop with an annoyingly cheap friend.** This is a particularly effective approach if the person is the type of cheapie who makes comments like "That costs only two dollars to make" and sighs every time you select something from the racks.

5. **Freeze your credit card.** This old savings trick really does work, but make sure you won't need the credit card anytime soon. I once had a very nasty incident thawing out the credit card in the microwave. Let's just say that credit cards aren't made of microwavable plastic.

Another way to save money is by saving your spare change. When I was a child, my father would often give me change from his pocket. I used to put this extra money into my Mickey Mouse bank. Although the Mickey Mouse bank is long gone, I continue to put pocket change in a little bank. Yes, I know it sounds corny, but your spare change could fund a pair of new shoes or help lead to an early retirement. At the end of each month lug your growing stash to the bank and deposit it in your shopping savings account to use at your whim. Whatever you don't use earns additional interest until you do use it.

Love a Store? Own a Piece of It!

Most financial whizzes encourage you to invest in what you know, so why not own a piece of your favorite store? As a shopper, the reasons you like a store are probably the same reasons others shop there. Budget favorites like Wal-Mart, Target, and the Gap are all publicly traded companies. Visit Yahoo! Financial and type in your favorite store(s) to see if they are publicly traded companies. Investing can be risky, so it may be a good idea to consult with a broker or other financial professional first.

Some of the Top Stores and Their Ticker Symbols*		
Store	**Ticker Symbol**	**Stock Exchange**
Amazon	AMZN	NasdaqNM
Bluefly.com	BFLY	NasdaqSC
The Gap	GPS	NYSE
Neiman Marcus	NMG-A	NYSE
Saks Fifth Avenue	SKS	NYSE
Target	TGT	NYSE
Wal-Mart	WMT	NYSE

NYSE = New York Stock Exchange

NASDAQ = National Association of Securities Dealers Automatic Quotation System

* This list is for informational purposes only and doesn't constitute an endorsement of the company or the stock by Kathryn Finney or TBF Group, LLC.

What's a Little Debt Among Friends?

Credit cards are not evil. It's the way we use credit cards that is evil. Prior to becoming a budget fashionista, I would use my credit cards to purchase the simplest of items—including nail polish. During my rebirth as The Budget Fashionista, I learned there is really only one simple rule when dealing with credit cards: no cash, no purchase.

We've all been tempted by the sweet prospects of deferred payment and the coupons for additional discounts you receive when you sign up for a store credit account. *Resist temptation!* Store-based credit cards tend to have higher interest rates than a regular Visa or MasterCard. Even if you open it just to receive the extra discount and pay it off at the end of the month, it still can negatively impact your credit report and credit score, which is often referred to as your FICO score.

Inside Scoop: *Financial Expert Debby Fowles*

Do you think a FICO score is the rating given to dogs at the Westminster dog show? No problem. Even experienced budgeters get confused by the term. Debby Fowles, the author of *The Everything Personal Finance in Your 20s & 30s Book* and *1000 Best Smart Money Secrets for Students* and About.com's guide to its Financial Planning site, explains the importance of FICO scores:

What is a FICO score?

Your FICO score, the most widely accepted credit score, is a three-digit number calculated by the Fair Isaac Corporation based on all the available data about you that indicates whether you're a good credit risk. Possible scores range from 300 to 850, with anything over 750 considered excellent and anything under 660 considered poor.

How are they calculated?

FICO scores are calculated using a complex formula that takes into account such things as how often you change jobs; whether you own your own home and how often you've moved; how many open credit accounts you have and the mix of types of credit accounts (credit cards, revolving loans, etc.); your combined credit limits and how much of your available credit you've used; your payment history, income, and education; what kinds of things you buy on credit; and a host of other data.

Why should a budget fashionista care?

FICO scores are now being used not only to decide whether to extend credit to you but also to determine the interest rate you'll receive on your mortgage, car loan, or other loans; the cost of your insurance premiums; whether a landlord will rent an apartment to you; and whether a potential employer will offer you a job. A low or borderline FICO score will cost you money in many areas of your life, so it pays to actively manage your score and keep it squeaky clean.

The True Cost of Credit			
Item	Retail Price	1 Year @ 12% Interest	Cost of Credit (After 1 Year)
Revlon nail polish	$5.99	$6.71	$.72
Gap basic T-shirt	$14.50	$16.24	$1.74
Old Navy stretch boot-cut jeans	$32.00	$35.84	$3.84
Pair of Seven jeans	$125.00	$140.00	$15.00
Coach small carry-all	$298.00	$333.76	$35.76
Manolo Blahnik strappy sandals	$515.00	$576.80	$61.80
Chloe blouse	$770.00	$862.40	$92.40
Roberto Cavalli silk dress	$2,875.00	$3,220.00	$345.00
Hermès ostrich Birkin bag	$13,900.00	$15,568.00	$1,668.00

So is there a time to use credit cards? Budget fashionistas should use credit cards only in the following cases:

- real-life emergencies such as emergency travel or car repairs (a sale at Neiman Marcus is not an emergency)
- to purchase basic, long-term necessities such as a good winter coat or a nice black interview suit (a sexy pair of Roberto Cavalli strappy heels to match your cocktail dress is not a necessity)
- to order products and services online because most credit cards offer buyer protection

Budget Fashionista Tip #4: Purchase a Gift Card

In order to track spending, purchase a Visa or American Express gift card (available online at www.visa.com, www.americanexpress.com, or at your local bank) to manage your shopping expenses. Just bring this gift card with you when you go shopping. Once the money is gone from the gift card, it is time to stop shopping. Many stores have implemented the gift card format for gift certificates, and I also find them particularly helpful for managing expenses. The cards are refillable, so you can add more funds when you are ready to go shopping again.

Don't fret if your budget is in the intensive care unit. In the next chapter you will learn some simple ways to infuse some life-sustaining money into your shopping accounts.

Chapter 2

Raising Some Dough: Ten Ways to Fund a New Wardrobe

In Chapter 1 you created a budget so stellar it would make Warren Buffet blush, and you probably discovered that you could use a little infusion of cash into your shopping savings account. This chapter gives you TEN Budget Fashionista–tested methods of raising funds for a new wardrobe—from selling old clothes to consignment shops to scoring a job as a mystery shopper. I'll also tell you how you and your friends can get a new wardrobe without paying a dime by throwing a clothing-swap party.

These methods have helped me add much-needed funds to my shopping savings account and have assisted me in cleaning out my closet. They by no means represent an exhaustive list of fund-raising options, so if you have a surefire way to raise additional funds that I didn't list in this chapter, please visit TheBudgetFashionista.com and share your method with other budget fashionistas.

Off to the closets!

1. Host a Clothing-Swap Party

A clothing-swap party is a gathering of like-minded fashionistas who want to get rid of the old and bring in the new—without spending a dime. Ideal for the weekend, these parties can be a great way to clean out your closet, spend some time with friends, and get new clothes for free. The first step in organizing a clothing-swap party is to send out invitations, making sure you send them at least two weeks prior to the party. You want to give your guests plenty of time to gather up their clothing and prepare for the event.

As you would with any good party, you need to make sure you have the right mixture of people. Invite people who wear similar sizes and have similar fashion tastes so that everyone has a great selection to choose from. For example, if you have a friend who wears a size 14, make sure there is at least one other person attending the party who wears a size 14. Also, don't make the mistake, as I did, of inviting someone who has a hang-up about secondhand clothes.

Think of your house or apartment as a mini department store, with each room representing a different kind of clothing. Divide the clothing and accessories into categories (outerwear, tops, etc.) and place them in separate rooms. You might want to dump all the shoes into your bathtub or use your kitchen, with its ample counter space, as the accessories department.

What You Need to Have a Clothing-Swap Party

- food
- music
- drinks
- a designated room or two—a living room and bedroom work best
- clothes—lots of glorious clothes

Things to Consider

1. The best time to have a clothing-swap party is during the change of seasons—such as March/April or August/September.
2. Keep the invitation list to no more than ten people to avoid any clothing-swap rumbles.
3. Set up specific ground rules. For example, you might want to say that all merchandise has to be wearable and clean with no major stains, holes, or rips. You might also want to have a game ready if two people want the same item. Rock-paper-scissors works well.
4. Be a good Samaritan and donate leftover items to your local

nonprofit thrift store. Be smart and keep the donation receipt for your taxes.

5. Have plenty of food and drinks on hand. Remember, this is a PARTY, so have fun.

2. Have a Garage Sale

My grandma Kathryn "Doonie" Hale is a member of the Garage Sale Hall of Fame. When I was a young shopper, Doonie and my mother and I would wake up early on Saturday morning, grab a newspaper, and head out to the local garage sales. Sometimes we found amazing treasures, sometimes we found only junk, but we always had fun.

Hanging out at local garage sales with my grandma taught me quite a bit about how to put one on successfully. According to Doonie, the most important step when putting together a garage sale is to determine the date. It's best to plan your sale for a weekend during warmer months. The nice weather encourages more people to be outdoors, translating into more customers for you. Unless you live in Miami, don't plan a garage sale for the dead of winter.

Curb appeal is also very important in putting together a successful garage sale. Think of it as the window display of your sale because most garage sale shoppers drive by the sale and assess the quality of the sale (the curb appeal) from their cars. Channel the spirit of famed window designer Simon Doonan of Barneys New York and put your best items out front, near the curb, to entice shoppers to your sale.

Budget Fashionista Tip #5: Call It an Estate Sale

If you are selling a large amount of high-quality jewelry and vintage furniture in good condition, calling your sale an estate sale will increase the number of customers and the amount you can charge for your items.

It's important to price your items to sell. People go to garage sales to find bargains—whether they are vintage, antique, or everyday household products. Many garage sale hosts fall into the trap of over-pricing items based on their sentimental value. For example, I went to a garage sale where the seller had slapped a $15 price tag on a lop-sided green vase made in a pottery class. Although I could under-stand the seller's pride at her crowning achievement in pottery, I knew the vase wasn't worth more than 50 cents. I immediately left the sale without looking at another item.

Once you've got your items priced and labeled to sell, you'll need to do a bit of merchandising by organizing them into cate-gories such as clothing, electronics, and kids. Set up several tables, benches, etc., to display the items. Again, make sure your best items are visible from the street.

A week or more before the sale, contact your local neighborhood newspaper to advertise it; many will give you free street signs to ad-vertise the sale because you placed an ad in their newspaper. Also, just before the sale, place several clearly marked signs with direc-tions around your neighborhood (but make sure you remove the signs after the sale). Have a friend test the directions out to make sure they work.

If you think you may not have enough stuff for a garage sale, hook up with friends and/or family. One year every woman in my family got together to hold one big garage sale in our backyard. We received well over $1,500 tax free. No garage? Then have a yard sale. No yard? Then have a sale in your apartment building or ask your management company or landlord if you can have a sale on the sidewalk outside your building.

Before setting up shop, check with your local municipal or city government to see if there are any special permits or licenses you'll need to have a garage sale.

Useful Tools for a Garage Sale

- round stickers from an office supply store
- Sharpie markers
- ad in a local neighborhood newspaper
- tables
- three workers—one cashier, one runner, and one overseer
- patience

Things to Consider

1. Create a spreadsheet of all the items you are selling, including price, item number, type of item, and, if there are multiple sellers, the owner's name. List item number along with the price on each item. This will make it easier to divide the proceeds once you're finished.
2. Place smaller items in bins according to price.
3. Be flexible and willing to negotiate.
4. Remember, you are competing with the local thrift shops and eBay. Check the price of similar items with these competitors and price accordingly.

3. Sell Designer Clothes to a Consignment Shop

At the end of each season I take inventory of my closet (you'll learn how to do this in "Chapter 5: Closet Inventory," page 62) and sell my underused high-quality designer clothes at a local consignment shop. A consignment shop is a retail store that sells goods on behalf of an individual or group for a percentage of the purchase price. With the rise in popularity of vintage fashion, selling your clothes at a consignment shop can yield big bucks for your shopping coffers without the time or effort of a garage sale.

Each consignment shop sets its own guidelines for the types of designers, styles, sizes, and quality they prefer. You and the consignment shop enter into an agreement by which the shop sells your goods for a selling fee, a percentage of the price. This fee usually runs between 40 and 70 percent. As with everything, this can be negotiated depending on the quality and the designer. For example, if you have a high-end Hermès bag you would like to sell, you could probably negotiate a lower consignment fee. Once your item is sold, the consignment shop deducts its fee and sends you a check for the balance.

Before consigning any items, make sure you receive a contract that spells out how much of the sale you will receive and the length of the contract (thirty, sixty, or ninety days). If you are leaving your items with the store, ask for the option to pick up any unsold items. Consignment boutiques often donate leftover items to local thrift stores. Always opt to pick up the item so that you get the tax benefit of the donation.

Useful Tools to Consign Your Items

- rolling bag to carry items
- an iron to prep the clothing

Things to Consider

1. Check clothing for stains, rips, or other damage and fix them prior to bringing the clothing to a shop. If an item is too damaged or stained to consign, throw it away.
2. Make sure you want to sell the item, or else you might find yourself purchasing the item from the store.
3. Negotiate with the store for lower consigning fees if you are selling a high-end designer item.
4. Try to consign only designer items or items that can be resold.

4. Sell Your Clothes in an Online Auction

Online auctions are a great way to make money by selling hard-to-find items like rare collectibles, high-end designer fashion pieces, and antique furniture. You can sell anything on online auction sites; the fast-food restaurant McDonald's once raised $75,100 for charity on Yahoo! Auctions by selling a prop french fry that "resembled" Abraham Lincoln (calling it the "Lincoln Fry"). I wouldn't suggest trying to find a food likeness of a former president to sell, but sites like eBay, Yahoo! Auctions, and Overstock Auctions do offer a simpler way to reach a larger audience than a garage sale or a local consignment shop. Even the nonprofit thrift store chain Goodwill has an online auction site.

Before posting your items on sites like eBay, Overstock, and

Inside Scoop: *Lynne and Donna Mastrilli, Consignment Store Divas*

Greene Street Consignment is one of the most popular and successful chains of consignment stores in Pennsylvania. It is owned by two consignment store experts and sisters, Lynne and Donna Mastrilli, who give us the inside scoop on how to consign your items.

How do consignment stores differ from a thrift shop?

Consignment is worlds different from thrift. Thrift stores tend to take a broader range of items, while consignment shops tend to be more selective. For example, we don't take items that are more than two years old, and all items must be in excellent condition—no musty odors or pet hair, and definitely no grandma stuff.

What are Greene Street's basic rules for consigning items?

Like most consignment stores, we have a minimum number of items that the owner must consign with us. At Greene Street there is a ten-piece minimum. We take Gap to Armani. But, again, very current items only. The entire process until the clothing hits the floor is three weeks long. The items are gone through initially by an employee, bagged, and dated. Three weeks later a store manager processes the consignment and may reject some or all of the goods. The customer then has the option to pick up rejected items.

Do you need an appointment?

Some shops require an appointment; however, there are several shops, like ours, that don't require one. It is always best to call before heading out to a store. Ask to speak with the store owner or manager. Ask what type of merchandise is usually consigned and whether or not your items would be accepted.

How are consignors paid?

At Greene Street the goods stay on the floor for sixty days with no markdowns, and the consignor is paid a 40 percent commission at the end of the term. There is also a VIP 50 percent program for long-standing customers with high-volume or designer merchandise.

Top Online Auction Sites and Their Seller Fees	
Online Auction Site	**Fees for Service**
Yahoo! Auctions (www.auctions.shopping.yahoo.com)	As of June 2005, Yahoo! Auctions no longer charges fees for *any* of its services, so you can auction your stuff for free.
Overstock Auctions (www.auctions.overstock.com)	Like eBay, Overstock Auctions charges a listing fee, fees for upgrades like bold titles, and a final value fee.
eBay (www.eBay.com)	eBay charges an insertion fee, which depends on the starting price of the item and whether or not you add additional services like extra pictures, bold titles, etc. If your item sells, eBay then charges a final value fee, which is a percentage of the final selling price. For more information go to the help center at eBay.com and key in "seller fees."

Yahoo! Auctions, take a seller's tutorial. It will give you a solid foundation on how to sell online, the mechanics of an auction, and any fees associated with listing your auction. It is important to understand how each auction system works so that you can maximize your profits.

One way to maximize your profits is to make sure you take several clear pictures of the item(s) you're selling. Think of yourself as an online retail store and present the item you're selling in the best possible way. Invest in a good digital camera—a 2- to 3-megapixel camera will do—to give the buyer a clear picture of the appearance and quality of the item.

Useful Tools for an Online Auction

- digital camera
- computer with Internet access (high speed is best)
- eBay, Yahoo!, or Overstock auction ID

Things to Consider

1. Research your product. Search for the product you are selling on the online auction site. Focus on auctions that have the highest bidders, observing how these sellers set up their auctions, the quality of their pictures, the way they describe their product, and starting price of their auctions.
2. Be honest. When describing your items, accurately describe any defects, blemishes, etc. Being honest will help build your representation as a seller.
3. Get a Paypal account. Paypal is the online money exchange system owned by eBay. It allows for quick, easy, and safe transactions between buyers and sellers. Note: Paypal does charge a small fee for processing transactions, but it makes selling online very easy.
4. Check your e-mail. Once your auction has started, you will start to get questions from prospective bidders. Always answer their questions promptly to ensure you get the maximum bid.
5. Ship quickly. Once payment is received and processed, ship quickly to avoid a negative seller rating.

You can also make money by selling items online for others by setting up your very own "consignment" shop on eBay. Visit eBay.com to find out how you can start and develop your own shop.

5. Get a Part-time Job at a Clothing Store

Imagine having access to the stockroom of your favorite store. Think about the power of having first shot at the latest sale items. Many budget fashionistas choose to score part-time or sometimes full-time jobs at their favorite stores to bring in extra money and receive the coveted employee discount.

The best time to find a position is during the holiday season—just in time for the post-holiday sales—or right after the summer season when the college students go back to school. The great part about working retail is that the hours are pretty flexible; you can work part-time on the weekends or weekdays after your main job. In addition, retail jobs, especially at big department stores, are open to all age groups—from high school students to retirees looking for supplemental income.

Budget Fashionista Tip #6: Avoiding the "Work and Spend" Trap

Be careful not to fall into the work and spend habit—spending your entire paycheck on purchases at the store where you work. To avoid this trap, opt for direct deposit of your check into your checking or savings account.

Useful Tools for Getting a Job at a Retail Store

- three business references
- résumé with most recent retail experience
- positive attitude
- neat, fashionable appearance

Things to Consider

1. Head to the store on a Monday or Tuesday. Stores usually aren't as busy early in the week, and the manager may be able to interview you on the spot.
2. Dress for the interview in a style that reflects the style of the store. If it's the Gap, wear clothing from the Gap to the interview. This will demonstrate that you understand and wear the product.
3. Make sure your part-time work doesn't conflict with your primary job. Some companies have "no moonlighting" clauses in their employee contracts.

The Budget Fashionista Explains:
How to Raise Money as a College Student

It's hard to be a fashionista with $3.56 in your bank account. That is exactly how much money I had in my checking account the second semester of my senior year of college as I stood face-to-face with a pair of black Charles David boots at Bloomingdale's. The boots cost $235, and in order to get them I needed a job.

During my college career, my bank account would often dip below freezing (less than $10). Usually I had a job or good old Mom or Dad to fall back on. After returning from a year abroad, the job was gone, and my parents were joyously celebrating the cutting of the proverbial financial umbilical cord. If I wanted those boots, then I was going to have to work.

Fortunately for me, there were, and still are, a plethora of employment options for shameless college students in need of additional shopping dollars. Here are a few of my favorites:

- **College/university annual giving fund.** Your college's annual giving fund is always hiring. It pays well because the job sucks. I used to play a game to see how many people would hang up on me in one night. My top score was twenty-one hang-ups in a row.

- **Psychiatry department or medical school.** Give to your fellow man! Become a test subject!

- **Dining hall.** This is one of the worst jobs, but there are some perks. A friend who was a dining hall attendant smuggled cakes, pastries, and the occasional pizza from the cafeteria to share with his dorm. He was later elected to a high position in student government.

- **Dorm room beautician.** If you're a gifted hair artist, earn extra money as a beautician in your dorm room. I made a pretty hefty sum braiding extensions into my friends' hair. Don't try this, however, if you have no experience working with hair.

- **National retail store.** Every college has a Gap within six blocks of the center of campus. It's the law. Since jobs there may be hard to come by, you may also want to try the Urban Outfitters down the street.

- **Live-in child-care worker or nanny.** Food, room, and occasional use of a car—it's like living at home, except you're hired help.

- **Temp agencies.** If you can alphabetize, you can temp. This is a great job because you can remain fairly anonymous while making a ton of money.

- **Grassroots organizations.** Fighting the power structure pays rather well. However, you will have to walk up to random people and explain the plight of the Northwestern spotted owl.

After my illustrious career as a member of the "annual giving" team, a couple of stints as a subject in the psych department, and weaving the heads of half my dorm, I was able to purchase the boots. Since it took me three months to save up the money, they were on sale for $125.

6. Sell Items at a Flea Market

Some shopping experts often compare flea markets to another famous market, the stock market, as places where deals are made, bargaining is done, and risks are taken. Flea markets are usually held outdoors in the parking lots of schools, churches, or racetracks, or in other open spaces. Some markets charge a small fee and require preregistration for a space, but most do not.

Buying and selling at flea markets has truly become an art form. Top sellers use guides like *U.S. Flea Market Directory: A Guide to the Best Flea Markets in All Fifty States* and travel from market to market selling both used and new items. I'm not suggesting that you pack up the RV and head across country selling your goods at local flea markets, but these guides provide useful tips on how to sell at flea markets and how to generate repeat customers.

Nowhere is the statement "One person's junk is another person's treasure" more true than at flea markets. Almost everything can be sold there—from household dishes to crafts to old clothes. At a flea market off the side of a road in Maryland, I once saw someone selling boxes of Kraft Macaroni & Cheese and old car tires at the same booth. Items need to be priced to sell, which means things must be sold at rock-bottom prices. As a seller at a flea market, you must be willing to negotiate.

Useful Tools for Selling at a Flea Market

- items to sell
- a portable table (card tables work well)
- cash (including lots of $1 and $5 bills and change)
- a box to use as a cash register
- market registration (if applicable)
- a boom box to draw customers to your table (although some markets don't allow them)

Things to Consider

1. Be prepared to negotiate. In order to run a flea market table, you must be flexible on the prices of your items.
2. If the market is outside, bring sunblock and a big beach umbrella to protect you and your items from the elements.
3. Visit www.fleamarket.com for more information on flea markets across the country.

7. Donate Your Old Clothes to Get a Tax Break

If you don't have the time to sell your old clothes online or get a second job, then donate your clothes to thrift stores like Goodwill and the Salvation Army. These stores depend on donations for their stock. Besides getting a nice tax write-off, you'll be helping to provide jobs to physically or economically challenged members of your community.

Remember, your local Goodwill is NOT your garbage can. Just because thrift stores readily accept your closet castaways doesn't mean they want garbage. Don't give dirty, smelly, ripped, or unrepairable clothing to your local thrift store.

Unlike consignment shops, thrift stores are usually run by nonprofit organizations. The tax break you get from donating is great, but the best part of giving your old items to them is that you are helping these charities generate supplemental funds to support their community service activities.

Donating to thrift stores is quite easy. Just clean out your closets and your garage, sort out the items that are in "wearable" condition, and place them in large plastic bags (lawn bags are best). Place the bags in your car and go to the nearest donation center. You should also check to see if they have a pickup service.

Useful Tools for Donating to a Thrift Store

- large plastic bags (lawn or garbage bags work best)
- old clothing
- optional: car or transportation
- a list of donated clothes

Things to Consider

1. Many thrift stores have pickup services for heavier items like furniture and electronics. Call ahead or check online for more information.
2. Some stores accept donations only during certain designated hours. Call ahead for donation hours.
3. Make sure you get a receipt for the items donated for your tax records.

8. Do It Yourself: Sell Craft Projects

If you have talent, why not turn your favorite hobby into a money-making venture? Join the Do It Yourself (DIY) movement and sell handcrafted items like scarves and hats to infuse some dollars into your shopping bank account.

DIY is a movement of aspiring designers who use their crafting skills to make unique one-of-a-kind fashions. Most DIYers build Web stores to sell their products. All you need to build a DIY website is a good Web design program like Macromedia Dreamweaver or Microsoft Front Page, a Paypal account (www.paypal.com) to process payments, and your crafty talent.

Superstars like Julia Roberts have made knitting the hottest hobby since Chia Pets. While knitting is a trendy activity, there are many other types of DIY projects that can be undertaken to make extra money, like scrapbooking. Many people would pay you to organize and create cute little books of their memories, some even paying more than $200 for a personalized scrapbook.

Useful Tools to Create and Sell Your Crafts

- talent (if you don't have this, skip to Method #9)
- digital camera (to take pictures of your work)
- Paypal account
- Web designer or a Web design program, Macromedia Dreamweaver or Front Page
- marketing plan

Things to Consider

1. You'll need to market your crafts in order to sell them. Start out by marketing them to friends and family members.
2. Think of a cool name for your store. DIY sites like Crafty Ass Chicks and Austin Craft Mafia have memorable names that help brand their products.
3. Join a DIY network such as Craftser.org for inspiration.

9. Mystery Shopping

Mystery shopping is a budget fashionista's ultimate dream. As a mystery or secret shopper you get paid to shop—conducting anonymous assessments of the services and products of a variety of institutions ranging from retail stores to banks. Not only is being a mystery shopper a smart way to make money, but it is also a great way to get free movie tickets, free food at restaurants, and even a free haircut. Called "shops," mystery shopping jobs pay between $10 and $150 (depending on the extent and time involved in conducting the assignment), and they include reimbursement for items purchased.

The Mystery Shopping Providers Association (MSPA) offers contacts to local mystery shopping companies. MSPA also offers certification and advance training for shoppers who want to qualify for higher paying jobs. For more information on becoming a mystery shopper, visit MSPA's website at www.mysteryshop.org.

When I first heard about mystery shopping, I thought it was just one big cruel joke played by evil credit card executives. Upon further investigation, however, I found that a budget fashionista could get paid to do what comes naturally. I searched for mystery shopping agencies online and signed up over the Internet.

Once approved, I was sent on my first assignment to a nationally franchised snack store and ordered its signature snack and a drink. Since eating is one of my favorite activities, I was excited to score free food. The job was to observe the cleanliness of the store, the customer service, and the taste of the snacks. I went into the store, ordered the snack, and was out in less than three minutes. Once home, I filled out a short form on my experience at the store and e-mailed it to the agency. Within a week, I was paid $10 plus the $3.55 I paid for the snack.

Useful Tools for Becoming a Mystery Shopper

- notebook to record observations
- Internet access to file reports and contact agencies
- Microsoft Word and Excel to complete the reports
- good writing and observational skills

Things to Consider

1. Although it's great to get paid to shop, remember that you are there to observe the service and/or the product. Don't spend time holiday shopping or, unless instructed, chatting with store employees.
2. Calculate the amount of time required for each project, including travel and report writing. Make sure the amount you're being paid for the job is worth your effort.
3. Check with the Better Business Bureau to make sure the mystery shopping firm is reputable.

10. Become a Personal Shopper

Although it's hard to believe, we all know people who hate to shop. These people usually get hives at the thought of entering a mall, or we see them wandering aimlessly around the store with no apparent sense of direction. Put these poor souls out of their misery and make money by offering to do their shopping for them. If you know people who work in the medical, legal, or banking fields — occupations that have very difficult hours and little flexibility in terms of time — you can offer to do shopping for them, saving them time and making yourself some money in the process.

A personal shopper usually charges either a percentage of the total amount of the items purchased plus expenses, or an hourly rate. As you build your client list, you can also make connections with stores and boutiques that are willing to give you a percentage of the sales you bring to the store.

The key to being a personal shopper is to know your clients and to anticipate what trends or styles will work for them. Remember, you are shopping for *them*, not for you, so it is important to focus on their style. You will need to know more than just where to shop. I suggest taking classes in image consulting, such as a course in color theory that will help you select the best colors for your clients. (For more information on classes near you, visit the Association of Image Consultants International online at www.aici.org.)

Useful Tools for Becoming a Personal Shopper

- a directory of stores in your area
- a separate banking account or credit card
- a class in wardrobe planning or image development
- clients

Things to Consider

1. You're shopping for a client, not for yourself. Focus on the client's needs.
2. Establish a separate bank account so that you don't confuse your funds with your client's funds.
3. Invest in the training. It will help you grow your business as well as help you network with others in the field.
4. Never, ever purchase items for a client without receiving payment for the items first. You don't want to be stuck with an item if the client decides not to purchase it.

Other, Not-So-Ethical Ways to Raise Shopping Dough

Now, if the previous suggestions don't work, you can always try these not-so-ethical ways of raising additional dough.

Marry rich. Marrying rich is a quick way to increase your shopping budget dramatically. If you're marrying just for money, however, you have to ask yourself if great clothes are worth a lifetime of unhappiness.

Become a sports mom or dad. Start your little one early in a high-paying sport like football, basketball, or baseball, and watch the dough start to pile up when he or she goes pro. Granted, your child may hate you, but you'll make a ton off your tell-all book.

Ask parents. This approach works particularly well if you're under thirty. (Trying this after thirty is pretty pathetic.) When going to visit your parents, wear the rattiest clothing, find shoes that "talk," and look like a general mess. Nine times out of ten they will be so mortified by your appearance that they will take you shopping. Don't ask Dad, however, to go into his 401(k) to help you pay for that Fendi baguette you've had your eye on.

Score celebrity friends. Celebrities get so much free stuff that most give it away to their friends, business partners, and housekeepers. Make sure you choose a celebrity friend who is your size and has your taste. If your style is more like Barbara Bush's, then having Kate Bush as a friend won't work very well.

Moving On

Step 1 gave you an overview of *what* you have to spend, but there is little value in knowing what you can spend if you don't understand *why* and *how* you should spend your hard-earned shopping dollars. "Step 2: Know Your Style" will teach you how to determine what you should spend your money on (your signature pieces, the Perfect Ten) and why it's important to focus your dollars on these items. You'll also learn more about my obsession with proper-fitting undergarments and what to do when your favorite item becomes a cliché.

Step 2

Know Your Style

Fashions fade, style is eternal.

—Yves Saint Laurent

*W*alk to your closet and open it up. If you are not immediately overcome by a sense of joy, you've got a big problem, and this step is going to fix it.

Most of our closets are as dysfunctional as a reality TV show family. The horrible state of our closets can be attributed to our roles as passive consumers. Celebrities, fashion magazines, and advertisements influence our purchases more than what makes us look our best. Think of the times you've bought something in a store after being persuaded by powerful advertising, a really good sale, or a commission-hungry sales associate, only to get home and realize you made a horrible mistake. You knew in the store that you weren't overly fond of the item, yet you still bought it, wasting time and money. You were being a passive consumer rather than actively selecting items that make you look and feel great. In Step 2 you'll uncover your own personal style and  learn to become your own personal stylist, key components of becoming a budget fashionista.

Chapter 3

Reality Dressing

The most important tool in uncovering your personal style is to practice reality dressing, which is dressing for who you are physically, emotionally, and financially at this point in your life—not who you were in college or how your favorite celebrity dresses. It's about knowing what looks good on you and understanding why it looks good on you. This is a basic concept that any budget fashionista can implement in her daily life. Throw out the fashion talking heads and use a little common sense. If you work as an administrative assistant for a busy executive in New York City, wearing four-inch Jimmy Choos is probably not the best idea. If you live in Minnesota and it's winter, who cares if pantyhose are "out"; there's nothing fashionable about frostbite. Don't wear short-short minis if you feel uncomfortable showing your legs. Don't wear dresses if you like to wear pants.

It can be difficult for normal women with very normal budgets to practice the concept of reality dressing at a time when wealthy celebrities with perfect bodies dominate all our images of style and beauty. Remember this: It's the job of stars to look great. If you had three hours a day to train with a high-end personal trainer named Gunnar, had your own South Beach–trained chef, and could afford to pay $18,000 for shiny white teeth, you, too, would look that good. The goal of reality dressing is to develop the BEST YOU, not turn yourself into some celeb clone.

Regardless of my size, I've always practiced reality dressing and take an honest look at my body because being honest with myself helps me look better. Like most women, I struggle with maintaining my girlish figure and couldn't be a size 2 if Dr. Atkins himself were my personal physician. Trying to wear a size 10 when you're really a 16 may make you feel better, but, trust me, it doesn't make you look better. Stylists have been known to request that designers change the label on a dress to a smaller size so that their customers will think they are smaller. Unfortunately, as your own client you need to check delusions of size grandeur at the door and practice a little reality dressing for yourself. Buying an item because it's a designer piece or because it's really cheap isn't worth it if it makes you look like a member of the Addams family. Make fashion fit your style.

Contrary to popular belief, fashion and style are not synonymous terms. Fashion is commercial, whereas style is personal. Fashion is *what* is "in," and style is *how* it is worn. Fashion is pants; style is culottes versus capris. Fashion is boot-cut jeans; style is Seven jeans versus Wrangler jeans. Good stylists use their incredible sense of style to interpret fashion to fit their clients.

Every style does not look good on everyone. With the exception of Lance Armstrong, there are very few people who look good in a pair of biker shorts. Not many women can rock a cone-breasted Gaultier corset like Madonna. Budget fashionistas not only know the top designers and the latest and classic trends, but they also have an acute sense of self. Knowing what looks good on your body and

General Fashion Do's and Don'ts	
Do . . .	**Don't . . .**
buy black. It's slimming and makes a cheap outfit look more expensive. Because it's a basic color, you can wear it more often.	always wear black. Add some color to diversify your wardrobe.
invest in good underwear that slims your tummy and shapes your butt.	intentionally let your thong show outside your pants.
wear pantyhose in the winter and to conservative offices.	wear pantyhose in the summer or if you live in a tropical environment.
use celebrities as style guides for developing your own personal style.	try to copy celebrities. Most celebrities don't look anything like their photos.
pay attention to the fabric of the garment. Good fabric almost always makes good clothes, but good clothes can never be made from bad fabric.	focus on the price so that you overlook the other important aspects of a garment, like style, fit, and fabric.
wear black shoes year-round.	wear white shoes after Labor Day unless you're a true fashionista, in which case by all means wear them.
focus on value, not necessarily price, when shopping for accessories like purses and shoes. Cheap-looking versions of these accessories can make a whole outfit look cheap.	pay a lot of money for accessories like earrings, necklaces, etc., unless they're your signature item.
buy sunglasses with UV protection on sale at outlet stores.	buy sunglasses without UV protection.
wear cool patterned stockings like fishnets.	wear white nylons with colored clothing. In fact, never wear white nylons. They look like surgical stockings and accent whatever flaws your legs have.

what makes you feel like a million bucks is as important as buying the item at a low cost.

Finding Your Body Shape

Measuring yourself is about as exciting as getting a root canal, but it is important to help you uncover your general body shape and to direct your focus toward styles that look good on you. To quickly assess your body type, do the following:

Find a measuring tape and measure yourself in the following three places: bust (around the fullest part of your chest), at your natural waist (not where you wear your low riders), and at your hips. Record these measurements in the chart below.

Your Measurements (in Inches)

Bust   _____

Waist   _____

Hips   _____

Budget Fashionista Tip #7: How to Find Your Natural Waist

With so many different types of pants and jeans, how does one find one's natural waist? Use this trick I learned from my seamstress grandmother. Stand up straight and bend your body to the side (either left or right) as if you are stretching for a workout. The crease, or the indentation between your hips and rib cage that is formed when you bend to the side, is your natural waist.

Use the measurements from above to determine your basic body shape from the chart on the next page.

Color: The Cheap Fix

Colors can have an extremely positive impact on your appearance and save you tons of money. You can get away with wearing black, white, and other neutral colors as often as needed without drawing attention to your limited closet. Color is also the cheapest way to camouflage figure issues. It is significantly cheaper than plastic surgery and carries few health risks. The guide on page 46 will help you choose colors that work best in your wardrobe.

Figure	Body Type	Body Shape
Bust, waist, and hips are proportionate (a noticeable difference between hips and waist, and waist and bust)	Hourglass or figure eight	
Bust is bigger than waist and hips	Inverted triangle	
Hips are bigger than waist and bust	Triangle	
Waist is bigger than bust and hips	Oval	
Bust, waist, and hips are about equal	Rectangle	

Color can also be used to hide problem areas and highlight positive areas, because the eye will travel to where the color is placed. To understand this concept take a red pen and place a dot on a piece of paper. Then take a black pen and place a dot on the same sheet. Look at the sheet. What dot does your eye notice first? Similarly, black is slimming because it absorbs light, making a shape seem smaller. On the other hand, white makes an object appear bigger because it reflects light, thus attracting the eye. However, wearing all black or all white is slimming because it creates a continuous line for the eye.

You're So Special: Petite and Plus Sizes

I have a big butt, which means I consistently tread the line between "normal" and plus sizes. So I understand the plight of the special-

Body Shape	How to Use Color
Hourglass or figure eight	Monochromatically, with a belt to emphasize shape
Inverted triangle	Darker colors on top and lighter colors on the bottom to help balance the figure
Triangle	Darker colors on the bottom and a bright-colored top to help balance the figure
Oval	Bright-colored heels with a pair of dark-colored flat-front pants will help elongate your body as well as draw attention away from your midsection
Rectangle	Monochromatically, with a bright-colored belt to help create a waist

size budget fashionista. Reduced to floor space the size of a child's closet, the special-size sections are so well hidden in stores that you have to be Jacques Cousteau to find them. Special-size budget fashionistas are penalized for being either too small or too big. Designers pay little attention to special sizes, and when they do, it is usually a muumuuesque top in hideous pastel colors or something you would find in the closet of an old maid.

So what's a special-size budget fashionista to do?

Fortunately, we no longer have to ride the "short yellow school bus" of fashion. There are solutions to our body concerns, and there are designers and stores that understand that being special doesn't mean we don't want to be stylish.

Petite Sizes

The tallest person I've ever met was actually probably one of the shortest persons I've ever met. As an exchange student living in Ghana during college, I lived next door to the Owusu-Ansah family. Auntie Dita was the matriarch of the family, a spirited Indian woman who was about four feet nine inches tall. At five feet ten inches, I was over a foot taller than her but never noticed she was short. Ever. She was always dressed to the nines and wore what I soon found out were three- to four-inch heels almost every day. She had a big personality and a keen fashion sense, and she wore her self-confidence like a $2,000 Balenciaga bag. A true budget fashionista.

Regardless of their actual height, petite fashionistas can make a powerful impact through their clothing. Like Auntie Dita, what you don't have in size you can more than make up for in style and presence.

Budget Fashionista Tip #8: Learn How to Walk in Heels

Don't know how to walk in heels? Rent the first season of the UPN television show *America's Top Model* and watch runway maestro Miss J. teach uncoordinated model newbies how to walk.

Things to Embrace

High heels. Wearing at least a two-inch heel will help elongate your body (both torso and legs).

A great tailor. A great tailor is an important asset because he or she can alter garments to fit your shape. (More about finding a great tailor later.)

Low-rise pants. Lower-waist pants will make your torso look longer. Make sure the hem of the pants hits about a quarter inch above the bottom of your shoe to give the illusion that your leg continues to the bottom of your shoe.

Big hair. Wearing your hair in a high bun or high ponytail will increase height as well.

Vertical stripes. These give the effect of looking taller.

Things to Avoid

Cropped anything. Cropped pants, tops, and jackets will shorten your torso.

Flat shoes. They will not give you the additional height you need.

Long unstructured skirts. They will drown your shape and make you look shorter. Hem the skirt to either three inches above your knee, at your knee, or three inches below your knee.

Miniskirts. Off-the-rack miniskirts will fall at an awkward length. Again, make sure your skirts fall either three inches above your knee, at your knee, or three inches below.

Where to Find Great Petite Fashions

The following stores and designers have great fashions for petite budget fashionistas.

INC.	trendy, bright, and affordable
Eileen Fisher	fluid fashions good for plus-size petites
DKNY	hip, younger urban wear
Ellen Tracy	a classic line, great for designer basics
Lily Pulitzer	sportswear for the ladies-who-lunch set
Lauren by Ralph Lauren	the classic American designer's preppy petite line
Anne Klein	suits and tops perfect for work
Gap	online store stocks a large number of petite-sized pants
Banana Republic	online store carries fashionable designs in petite styles
Dana Buchman	higher-end fashions for petite fashionistas

Visit TheBudgetFashionista.com for more information on these designers and stores.

Plus Sizes

The era of flower-printed muumuus is long gone. The fashion caste system that separated people into "those who can" (skinny and rich) and "those who can't" (everyone else)—which waas created by snobby designers and power-hungry fashion editors (who, by the way, are often plus-sized themselves)—is crumbling. A new fashion utopia is emerging that has several fashion options for curvy fashion-istas, none of which involve polyester tent dresses. In this diet-obsessed, waif-model culture, designers still gear their creations toward a size 4, and their version of a plus size is to simply make a bigger size 4. Commit the size rules below to heart and watch your style quotient rise as you learn to shop in the stores that enhance your voluptuous fashionable self. Take that, Kate Moss!

Budget Fashionista
Explains: Avoid Horizontal Lines

Both plus-size and petite fashionistas should avoid horizontal stripes. Horizontal lines make you look wider because they draw the eye from left to right. Focus on wearing vertical lines, which make you look thinner because they draw the eye from top to bottom. That being said, one of my favorite tops is a rainbow-striped Isaac Mizrahi shirt I purchased for $12.99 at Target. In order to counteract its widening effect, I wear it underneath a jacket, which makes the horizontal lines look shorter.

Things to Embrace

Dress monochromatically. Dressing in one color deemphasizes your problem areas by creating one long silhouette. This works with any color, not just black.

Wear heels. Heels elongate your legs, making you look slimmer in the process.

Put on a blazer with a belt. Throwing a blazer or cute jacket over a pair of belted pants and shirt makes your waist look smaller because the eye can't see how far the waist extends.

Get measured for a bra. Wearing the right bra size can make you look thinner. Experts say that more than 80 percent of women wear the wrong bra size, and a large percentage of plus-size women do so because they're embarrassed to wear the larger sizes. If a garment bulges or shows your "rolls," either it doesn't fit or you are wearing the wrong bra size.

Stick with boot-cut pants. They have a slight flare at the bottom that creates a more balanced look.

Purchase collared and V-necked shirts. Both are very slimming.

Wear vertical stripes. They are slimming and make you appear taller.

Utilize thinner fabrics that drape. Heavier fabrics add bulk to your frame.

Budget Fashionista Tip #9: A Little Spandex Can Go a Long Way

For those of us who need a little support, jeans and pants that have a spandex content of 2 to 5 percent are best. (Any higher, and you will look like you belong in an aerobics class.)

Things to Avoid

Low low-rise pants. Even though low-rise pants can be quite flattering on plus-size figures by elongating the torso, they can create a "roll" effect. Unless you live on a beach in Rio de Janeiro, skip the ultra-low-rise pants.

Cropped jackets. Cropped jackets draw attention to your waist and butt. Purchase well-structured jackets that hit you right below your bottom or longer trench coats.

Horizontal stripes. They widen the body.

Where to Find Great Plus-Size Fashions

Lane Bryant isn't the only place for plus-size fashionistas to find great deals to fill their style quotient. Here are some other great designers.

Ashley Stewart	fashion-forward pieces, most priced under $40
AbbyZ	hip but very expensive; sold at stores like Lord & Taylor and Saks Fifth Avenue
Lafayette 148	one of my favorite designers, also hip and expensive; can be found on sale at Off 5th, Saks Fifth Avenue Outlet, and Last Call Neiman Marcus
Tom and Linda Platt	beautiful evening dresses up to size 4X
Carmen Marc Valvo	sexy evening wear
INC	trendy, bright, and affordable
Eileen Fisher	fluid fashions good for plus-size petites
DKNY	stylish urban wear that younger plus-size fashionistas will want to check out
Linda Allard for Ellen Tracy	one of the best career lines for plus-size fashionistas
Old Navy	the cheaper cousin to the Gap that has an extensive plus-size section with most items well under $30
Ralph Lauren	the classic American designer's preppy plus-size line
Anne Klein	stylish suits for work
The Gap	online store (www.gap.com) stocks pants up to size 20 and tops up to size XXL

Tommy Hilfiger   hip mixed with classic; the plus-size line is great for weekend wear

Dana Buchman   great, albeit expensive line

Sunny Choi   chic, fashionable evening wear and suits

Visit TheBudgetFashionista.com to learn where to find these designers and stores.

Chapter 4

Finding Your Personal Style

In this chapter are two exercises to get you thinking about your personal style. Most of us have a variety of styles, so don't fret if you find that you don't fit into one particular category. It's fine to mix styles. For example, during the winter I dress in bright colors and layered sweaters to brighten my mood, evoking a sort of bohemian look. During the summer, however, I prefer to combine trendy and socialite looks. Mixing styles will help you create your own personal style.

BUDGET + FASHION
= SHOPPING!

Exercise 1: Personal Style Quiz

The following quiz will help you uncover your personal style. This is not the SATs and there are no right or wrong answers, so don't get all clammy. Just select the answer that best fits the way you view your style.

1. Select the line with the words that best describe your personality.
   a. active, friendly, casual, athletic
   b. spontaneous, trendsetter, label-aware, bold
   c. organized, efficient, conservative, consistent
   d. demanding, sophisticated, confident, well groomed
   e. adventurous, creative, techie, futuristic
   f. sensuous, romantic, supportive, understanding

2. Imagine it is the end of the world, and you get to choose one dream outfit to wear. Choose the line that best describes the outfit you would choose.
   a. a polo shirt, low-rise jeans, sneakers, and small diamond studs
   b. Jimmy Choo's pointed toe boots with four-inch stiletto heels, Dolce & Gabbana jean skirt, a cropped Juicy Couture hooded fur jacket, C&C California tee, and Gucci sunglasses
   c. pair of plain-front gabardine slacks with matching top and a comfortable pair of flats
   d. bouclé suit, pearls, two-inch Ferragamo pumps, and a Louis Vuitton Doggie bag with Fernando, your perfectly groomed pet Maltese, inside
   e. cropped cargo pants, a "Free Trade My Butt" T-shirt, pair of streetwear Pumas, a bright orange messenger bag (to carry your laptop, of course), and an iPod
   f. a floor-length pink silk skirt, cropped, scoop-necked cream T-shirt, a pair of sequined sandals, lace headband, and pearl drop earrings

3. Your aunt Mattie, who gives the worst gifts in the world, just sent you a birthday gift. You start to feel nauseous as you take out:
   a. a boxed set of makeup from Lancôme
   b. a $500 gift certificate to Goodwill
   c. a T-shirt that reads "I'm a Bad Bitch"
   d. a jogging suit from the Jacquelyn Smith line at Kmart
   e. a ticket to a Tony Robbins seminar
   f. a pair of Nike sneakers

4. Your significant other is planning a special night out for your three-month anniversary. He or she asks your friends to select the perfect concert to take you to. Which of the following do they suggest?

a. Avril Lavigne, Sum 147, and Maroon 5
b. 50 cent, Nelly, and J. Lo
c. Clay Aiken, Mormon Tabernacle Choir, and Charlotte Church
d. Yo-Yo Ma, Leontyne Price, and the New York Philharmonic
e. Sarah McLachlan, John Mayer, and Norah Jones
f. Fleetwood Mac, Air Supply, and Chicago

5. You have a nervous breakdown at the office copy machine because the machine just won't collate, and your boss forces you to take a vacation. Where do you head to?
   a. Vail
   b. Miami's South Beach
   c. Disney World
   d. Saint-Tropez
   e. Amsterdam
   f. local bed and breakfast

6. Your mom had a nice long talk with Aunt Mattie, and this year she sends you a gift that you actually want. Your eyes well with tears as you open a complete outfit from which of the following designer lines?
   a. Lily Pulitzer
   b. Juicy Couture
   c. St. John
   d. Chanel
   e. Marc Jacobs
   f. Nanette Lepore

7. After years of coaching, your husband has finally figured out what gifts to get you for your birthday. He wants to give you something special, so he heads to which of the following?
   a. Sports Authority
   b. Barneys New York
   c. Talbots
   d. Saks Fifth Avenue
   e. Urban Outfitters
   f. Laura Ashley

8. Your idea of a perfect Friday night consists of:
    a. watching the local sports team
    b. hitting the clubs
    c. participating in a community sing-along
    d. heading out to a charity ball
    e. attending a lecture
    f. watching a romantic foreign film

9. You are at the mall and decide to pick up a new pair of shoes. What do you purchase?
    a. a pair of sneakers
    b. four-inch stiletto heels
    c. ballerina flats
    d. designer pumps
    e. designer street sneakers
    f. espadrilles

10. What television show most describes your life?
    a. *ESPN Sports Center*
    b. *Sex and the City*
    c. *Seventh Heaven*
    d. *Dynasty*
    e. *The Real World*
    f. *Dr. Quinn, Medicine Woman*

11. You are getting ready for a hot date. You open your lingerie drawer to put on:
    a. a sports bra
    b. nothing; you don't wear underwear
    c. a sensible basic black bra
    d. La Perla matching panty and bra set
    e. whatever underwear your mom sent you
    f. lacy bra and thong set

Tally up your answers by counting how many of each letter you circled. Don't worry if your answers are scattered. That just means you like a hybrid of different styles. In general, if you answered:

Mostly A: Sporty. You tend to drift more toward sporty styles. This doesn't mean you live in tracksuits—you've been known to rock the occasional dress—but comfort and movement are more important to you than the latest frilly style. You're a carefree, low-maintenance fashionista who wants a quick and easy style. Polo shirts, jeans, slouch pants, khaki pants, cotton sailor pants, workout clothes, canvas sneakers, and riding boots are all types of sporty clothing. Backpacks, key chains, and baseball caps are some examples of sporty accessories.

When developing your closet as a sporty, focus on purchasing items that have a casual bent and are functional. Find clothing that has a more menswear cut to it, loose and flowing with a bit of structure—an example is flat-front, loose-fit pants that sit slightly below your waist. Head to the menswear section of your local department store to study the fabrics used for their clothing and then try to find similar fabrics in the women's section.

WHERE TO SHOP: Look for pieces from companies like Lacoste, J. Crew, Lady Foot Locker, Lily Pulitzer, Baby Phat, Tommy Hilfiger, Old Navy, and the Gap. Shop at stores like Marshalls, Lady Foot Locker, and most major department stores. Your celebrity style twins are Serena Williams, Ellen DeGeneres, and the late, great Katharine Hepburn.

Mostly B: Trendy. Girl, you have the uncanny ability to wear every trend—at the same time. You scour every fashion magazine you can find for the latest fashions and faithfully read the *New York Post*'s Page Six even though you live in Kansas.

To keep abreast of the latest trends, make sure you have subscriptions to celeb magazines, like *In Style* and *Life & Style*. Also read "The Look Book" section at NewYorkMagazine.com to get the scoop on what trendsetters are wearing. Pay close attention to shows such as *Fashion Police* on the Style Network to keep abreast of the do's and don'ts of being trendy.

WHERE TO SHOP: Sashay to the local hip boutique for the latest from trendier designers and stores such as Dolce & Gabbana, Versace, and Roberto Cavalli. In the mall go to Forever 21, Express, H&M, Bebe, Debs, and Torrid. Your celebrity style twins are Beyoncé, Gwen Stefani, and Jessica Simpson.

Mostly C: Conservative. You're a little more conservative than other fashionistas. People often confuse your conservative personal style as lack of interest in shopping and fashion. In fact, you love fashion and style just as much as other fashionistas but prefer that people pay more attention to your personality than to your clothing. Your dress reflects your more conservative nature (although there are times you get a little wild—like at the office Christmas party).

Clean, straight lines and classic colors like navy blue, gray, black, and beige should dominate your closet (although you should also have a couple of fun pieces that we'll talk about later). Focus on filling your closet with investment pieces because the "latest" styles will most likely lie dormant in your closet.

WHERE TO SHOP: Look for clothes from designers such as Ralph Lauren, Liz Claiborne, Donna Karan, Sigrid Olsen, and Calvin Klein. In the mall look for stores like J. Jill, Talbots, and Lord & Taylor. Buy tailored suits, simple collared shirts, and other types of career wear in classic colors. Your celebrity style twins are Hillary Clinton, Candice Bergen, and Jennifer Connelly.

Mostly D: Socialite. You dream of the day you'll be able to afford couture Chanel, and you long to be featured in *Town & Country* magazine. Groomed down to your perfectly pink toenails, everything you wear screams money (even though you got it from the local consignment shop).

The key to maintaining your socialite style is to remain always polished. Everything you put on your body must have a purpose and convey a sense of status. That is why most fashionistas with socialite style are members of the frequent buyers club at their local knockoff mecca. Resist the urge to purchase knockoff junk, especially the Louis Vuitton Monogram bags. Instead, put extra money in your shopping savings account to purchase real designer bags from Longchamp, Mulberry, and other high-end designers.

WHERE TO SHOP: Your best designers and stores are Chanel, Club Monaco, The Limited, Lanvin, Oscar de la Renta, Nine West, Last Call Neiman Marcus, Off 5th, Saks Fifth Avenue Outlet, and Givenchy. You should also shoot for quality designer-inspired pieces like bags from Hype or cubic zirconia earrings with silver posts, rather than low-quality fakes with a designer's name splattered everywhere. Look for four-ply cashmere sweaters from Lord & Taylor, designer suits by Chanel at your local consignment shops, and "designer-like" evening dresses from ABS Allen Schwartz. Also check out the mass-market designer lines such as A Line by Anne Klein at Sears and Isaac Mizrahi's line for Target. Ivanka Trump (daughter of Donald Trump), Nicole Kidman, and Sarah Jessica Parker are perfect celebrity style twins for you to follow.

Mostly E: Urban Trekker. Whether you live in the heart of the big city or in the suburbs, you look like you stepped right off the nearest subway. Your favorite films are documentaries, and you've been known to stay home for a good Bill Moyers special on PBS. Your closet is mostly full of jeans, cargo pants, messenger bags, puffy jackets in bright colors, cotton-ribbed tank tops in a variety of colors, designer casual sneakers, and comfortable boots from manufacturers like Frye.

Technology is a major part of an urban trekker's personal style. Carrying the latest iPod is more important to you than having the latest designer purse, so look for clothing that is constructed with an almost architectural feel, with tons of pockets for your tech needs. When purchasing handbags, look for large totes that can double as laptop cases.

WHERE TO SHOP: Your best fashions come from Urban Outfitters, Marc by Marc Jacob, the Thalia line at Kmart, Dsquared, Levi, Mossimo, Anna Sui, Parallel by BCBG at Sears, Diesel, and Blue Plate. Your celebrity style twins are Alicia Keys, Angelina Jolie, and Cameron Diaz.

Mostly F: Romantic. You hold Meg Ryan movie marathons at your house and cried when "Bennifer" broke up. You love to wear lace and long flowing skirts, and your cedar-lined hope chest is full of Frette linen. You also love velvet, wide-leg pants, floral prints, crocheted shirts, and empire waist dresses.

Your clothing should communicate a sense of openness, compassion, and warmth, so think soft and feminine when building your wardrobe. Choose fabrics like chiffon, silk, and high-quality rayon that drape fluidly on the body.

WHERE TO SHOP: Your best designers and stores are Nanette Lepore, Catherine Malandrino, Cynthia Steffe, and Tracy Reese. While at the mall, shop at Arden B., Cache, and Rampage. Also try these online and catalog companies: Victoria's Secret, Newport News, and La Redoute.com. Look to Jennifer Lopez, Kate Hudson, and Goldie Hawn for style guidance.

Exercise 2: Using Magazines

In this exercise you will need to purchase major fashion magazines such as *Vogue, Glamour, InStyle, W, Life & Style Weekly,* and *Marie Claire.* Randomly circle all the items you love and would purchase, regardless of price. Using the style descriptions from the quiz, count up all the different styles you have circled and place the totals in the chart below.

Style	Number of Items Circled
Sporty	
Trendy	
Conservative	
Socialite	
Urban Trekker	
Romantic	

The Results

Take the results from this chapter's two exercises and enter the styles with the most items circled in the spaces below.

My personal style from exercise 1: _____

My personal style from exercise 2: _____

My personal style is: _____

The above exercises are just to get you thinking about your personal style. As I stated at the beginning of this chapter, many of us have multiple personal styles. Remember to mix these styles to create your own personal style. For example, if your style is trendy but your work environment is conservative, pair a stylish camisole with your basic business suits or carry a bold bag. If your personal style is romantic but you live in a big city, pair a floral print Western-style shirt with a pair of cargo pants. Your goal is to create a personal style that is uniquely yours and to develop a closet full of pieces that you love and wear.

Chapter 5

Closet Inventory

Closets are like extremely fashionable pets: They need to be fed, cleaned, and loved. When you're your own personal stylist, it is your job to nurture your closet in order to maximize your shopping dollars and your outfit possibilities. I suggest that at the beginning of every season you go through your closet systematically and conduct a closet inventory, separating the bad from the good, the stained from the spotless, and the unbecoming from the flattering. The process is tedious but gratifying because you'll end up with a more orderly closet. This effort requires an entire day (or sometimes an entire weekend) and helps you assess the gaps in your closet.

Conducting a closet inventory is an important step in becoming a budget fashionista because it helps you focus your limited shopping budget on pieces that will help you expand your closet. By the end of this chapter you will be able to create a detailed shopping list to place in your "look book" that will help guide your purchases in "Step 3: Know Your Bargains" (page 149).

Before you begin your inventory, take a moment to think about your five favorite items in your closet right now.

Here are my five favorite items:

1. Turquoise rope necklace from the Salvation Army. The color really brightens my face and shows off my personality. Plus, it cost only 25 cents.

True Shopping Confessions:
What's the Most Expensive Thing in Your Closet?

Sometimes you just need to splurge. However, one person's splurge could be another person's budget. To find out more on this topic, I asked readers of my site to name the most expensive item in their closet:

"A $40 wool coat from the army surplus store. I spruced it up myself, and it is the warmest coat ever."

"A $15,000 mink coat."

"A green satin cocktail dress from the Banana Republic outlet on clearance for $60."

"A cashmere wrap sweater by Christopher Fischer. It was originally $400, but I got it for $45."

"My long, black, fully-lined wool winter coat. I paid $250 for it, and it was from the Burlington Coat Factory."

"A red leather Prada miniskirt that cost 350 Euros. But I got it at the outlet in Florence, Italy, so I should still get the budget fashionista credit!"

"A Worthington pea coat from JC Penney for $100."

2. Burberry trench coat from the Burberry Outlet. This coat makes me feel like Kate Moss walking down a cobblestoned street in London.
3. Black wide-leg dress pants from Nine West. These pants are incredibly comfortable, and the wide leg balances my hips.
4. Old Navy Perfect Fit T-shirts. I wear these shirts almost every day.

5. Black Kenneth Cole flats from the outlet. I love these shoes more than I love chocolate because they're incredibly comfortable and classic in an Audrey Hepburn sort of way.

Now list your five favorite items below and explain why these items are your favorites.

Favorite Items	Why It Is My Favorite Item
1.	
2.	
3.	
4.	
5.	

Don't worry if nothing in your closet gets your juices flowing. By the end of this book you'll be well on your way to having a closet full of love.

How to Clean Out Your Closet

You've identified your five favorite items, and now it's time to clean out the junk. Create the following four piles and place each of them in a different corner of the room so that the piles don't mix.

Pile 1: Clothing you never wear but could sell on eBay or at a consignment shop, particularly well-known designer pieces. Place these items in a large suitcase or carrying bag.

Pile 2: Clothing that you hate, never wear, and frankly are a bit embarrassed that you own. These should head straight to Goodwill. Place these items in a large garment bag.

Pile 3: Clothing you actually wear and is in great condition. These clothes stay in your closet.

Pile 4: Clothing you would wear but needs to be altered, hemmed, or otherwise fixed. Place these in a laundry bag.

Put the Goodwill bag in the backseat of your car (not your trunk, or you'll forget to take it there). If you sew, place the alteration bag by your sewing machine. Otherwise place the bag next to your dry cleaning so you'll remember to take it with you when heading to the cleaners.

Although every closet should have a few trendy pieces, you should always follow the 70-30 rule: Seventy percent of your closet should be staples such as black pants, a killer pair of jeans, a black suit, a pair of tennis shoes, etc. These are things that you will keep for a long time and that almost never go out of style. They include staple versions of your signature piece as well. The other 30 percent should be trendy, up-to-date pieces. Spend little money on these pieces because they will quickly go out of style.

The Budget Fashionista Explains: The Perfect Ten, the Things That Should Be in Every Closet

"I have nothing to wear." If you hear yourself uttering this statement frequently, you have a dysfunctional closet. Your closet is probably missing several key pieces that would allow you to transition easily from one outfit to the next. It's time to stop the insanity and learn to build a functional closet.

The Perfect Ten are the classic pieces that should be in every woman's wardrobe. It's truly amazing the number of outfits that can be made from having them in your wardrobe—at least thirty-two different outfit combinations. Along with your signature item, the majority of your shopping dollars should be spent on purchasing classic, well-made versions of the following items that fit your personal style.

Black suit. If you invest in only one item, invest in a tailored black suit. One black suit jacket with either a matching black skirt or black pants is a must for any budget fashionista closet. Look for black suits made of a medium-weight fabric such as gabardine for year-round wear.

White cotton dress shirt. This is an important closet staple that can be both trendy (worn underneath your favorite T-shirt) and classic (worn with a business suit).

Pair of plain black pumps. A pair of 1½- to 3-inch plain black pumps can take you from the office to dinner. It's easy to change the appearance of these shoes by adding shoe jewelry, available at most shoe stores and department stores like Nordstrom.

The perfect pair of jeans. A great-fitting pair of jeans should be standard in every closet. Two pairs are even better. You don't have to spend a small fortune for these. Both the Faded Glory and the Rider brands are great-fitting jeans that cost less than $30.

Little black dress. This dress should be made of a seasonless, sturdy lightweight fabric such as a cotton-rayon blend. Avoid heavy fabrics like wool and thick cotton that counteract the slimming effects of the black color.

How to Wear the Perfect Ten

Eight Quick Dressy Outfits		
Top	**Bottom**	**Shoes**
Trench coat and white dress shirt	Black skirt	Black pumps
White cotton dress shirt	Khakis	Black pumps
Black blazer and black dress		Black pumps
Trench coat		Black pumps
Black blazer and white top	Khaki pants	Black pumps
Spandex T-shirt	Black suit pants	Black pumps
Black suit		Black pumps
Trench coat and black dress		Black pumps

Eight Quick Casual Outfits		
Top	**Bottom**	**Shoes**
Trench coat and white dress shirt	Jeans	Sneakers
Fun color T-shirt	Khakis	Sneakers
Trench coat and spandex T-shirt	Jeans	Sneakers
Black blazer and white T-shirt	Jeans	Black pumps
Spandex T-shirt	Jeans	Sneakers
White T-shirt	Black pants	Sneakers
White T-shirt	Black skirt	Sneakers
Black T-shirt	Black pants	Sneakers

Spandex T-shirts. Purchase a form-fitting (not tight-fitting) spandex T-shirt in black, white, and a fun color. Perfect for layering as well as wearing alone, these shirts help stretch your closet far beyond its limits. The Old Navy Perfect Fit stretch T-shirt is a great brand.

Leather tote bag. A sturdy tote serves two functions: a briefcase during the week and a shopping bag for the weekends.

Pair of sneakers. Purchase a pair that can be worn for workouts and for casual shopping days.

Trench or all-weather coat. These can be used as a coat and as a dress. Look for a coat with a removable lining so that you can increase usage.

Khaki and chino pants. These pants add diversity to your outfits.

Although the above items are classic pieces, focus on purchasing versions of the pieces that fit your own personal style. For example, I tend to be a little more conservative when looking for my Perfect Ten, so when looking for a trench coat, I purchased the classic Burberry trench. If your personal style skews more toward Urban Trekker, you might want to look for a version of the classic coat by a designer like Marc Jacobs. If your style is Romantic, you may want to look for a black skirt suit with a flutter skirt and figure-skimming jacket rather than a black pantsuit with a classic two-button blazer that might interest someone with a Sporty style. Adding individuality to your Perfect Ten helps you maintain your own sense of style while creating a functional closet.

Take the clothes from pile 3 and, using the form on the next page, record whether you have these staples in your closet.

Analyze the form to see where you need to target your shopping budget. If you're missing any of these staples, your shopping dollars should be focused on purchasing them before adding other pieces. In Step 3 we will discuss where to find these pieces for a steal.

Branching Out

Once you've added the above items to your closet, you can start to add other pieces to your wardrobe. Find another classic suit in a

Closet Inventory Form: Staples		
Perfect Ten	**Yes**	**No**
Black suit (with pants and/or a skirt)		
White cotton dress shirt		
Plain black pumps		
Perfect pair of jeans		
Little black dress		
Spandex T-shirts		
Leather tote bag		
One pair of sneakers		
Trench or all-weather coat		
One pair of khakis or chino pants		

neutral color like gray or brown, look for a great cardigan or a classic twin set, and invest in a good pair of black or brown leather boots. You might want to keep your eye out for a jean jacket or, if you're more formal, a casual blazer. Last but not least, make sure your closet has at least four trendy pieces that work with your body type.

Although having the Perfect Ten and other staple items in your closet will help you to stretch your wardrobe, you also need to make sure your wardrobe is balanced. Every budget fashionista should strive to have at least two tops for every pair of pants because you can wear pants more times than tops. If your ratio is a bit off but you have the above basics, focus your shopping expenditures on purchasing more tops to balance out your closet.

There are times when you should purchase multiple quantities of an item, like if it is an item that is normally hard to find. I have a hard time finding pants that fit my very curvaceous figure, so when I find a brand of pants that fit, I buy at least two pairs. Also, purchase multiple quantities of items you tend to wear a lot—like jeans, black pumps, etc.

For more information on developing a functional closet, including a clothing-size chart, head to TheBudgetFashionista.com.

Closet Inventory Form: Additional Items		
Item	Yes	No
Another pair of great-fitting jeans		
Knee-length skirt		
Black or brown leather boots		
Cardigan or classic twin set		
Classic suit in a neutral color		
Casual blazer or jean jacket		
One pair of sexy strappy heels		
Winter coat (if applicable)		
Four or more trendy pieces		

Taking Care of Your Closet

The truly fabulous know that an often overlooked aspect of looking great on a budget is knowing how to take care of one's clothing. Every budget fashionista should know at least one good tailor, know their way around a washing machine, and know the address of a great dry cleaner. Resist the urge to throw out the clothes you put in Pile 4—keepers that need to be fixed. Yes, it may be easier, but it isn't necessarily cheaper to give them to the local thrift store. Think of it this way: Paying $10 for a tailor to fix the hem of your favorite Tahari skirt is much cheaper than buying a completely new skirt.

A good tailor is a budget fashionista's secret weapon. Having a good tailor who knows your body type and your style can give you more options when it comes to budget shopping. Tailors are able to reclaim the glory days of old garments by strategically placing a nip or tuck—making sale rack finds fit like a glove and turning thrift store finds into closet staples. Fabulous tailors and seamstresses can also create original or knockoff pieces from some of your favorite designers for a fraction of the cost.

Most of us dream of having our very own personal tailor. You don't have to be a star or have a star's bank account to get tailor-made clothes. Head to your local community college or fashion school, visit your dry cleaner, or check at the local fabric store for a seamstress or tailor who can re-create designer looks for you at a reasonable price.

Take Care of Your Own Clothes

Knowing how to take care of your own clothes can save you a ton of money on dry cleaning, alterations, and clothing-replacement costs. For example, you can unshrink a wool sweater using warm water and hair conditioner. See the box on the next page for instructions on how to fix common laundry problems yourself.

Budget Fashionista Tip #10: Take Care of Your Clothes Like a Stylist

Below are some tricks used by fashion and celebrity stylists to help preserve and care for the clothing entrusted to their care. Use these tricks to help maintain the clothes in your closet.

Iron with steam. Every budget fashionista *must* have an iron. No exceptions. I'm not talking about an industrial-strength heavy steel one but a simple iron with steam. The steam will help you press out deep creases and prolong the life of your clothes by reducing the use of starch. You can find a good steam iron for under $20 at your local Target or Wal-Mart. Whenever possible, try to use distilled water in your iron; it will extend the life of the iron.

Double-stick tape. This tape has adhesive on both sides. Stylists use it to stick clothing safely to the skin. This works great for plunging necklines; think J. Lo and the infamous Versace dress. Although most stylists use the brand Top Stick, you can also use double-stick tape purchased at a local wig shop or Scotch-brand double-stick tape. In order for it to work effectively, your skin needs to be free of lotions and oils.

Problem	Solution
Shrunken wool sweater	Stretch the sweater by soaking it in a tub of gentle hair conditioner (about a quarter-size amount) and lukewarm water for approximately 15 minutes. Do NOT wring. Drain the water from the sink. Gently press the sweater against the sink walls to remove water from the garment. Remove the garment and lay it flat on a towel. Use another towel to blot the excess water away. Gently pull the sweater into the desired shape (called blocking).
Bleeding from another garment	Rinse the stained garment immediately with cold water and wash again with detergent.
Dirt on cuffs of pants	Add a little water to a cup of powder detergent and mix until it forms a paste. Apply the paste to the dirt spots and let sit for 10 minutes. Rinse thoroughly. If this doesn't work, you can turn them into cropped pants by cutting the pants approximately 2 inches above your ankle.
Bleach stains	Sew patches or appliqués over the stain. For black garments, try to color in the stain with a black Sharpie marker.

Masking tape. Stylists use electrical and masking tape to protect the soles of expensive shoes from horrible scuffs (cream for cream- or white-bottomed shoes and black for black shoes). Following the outline of the sole, apply pieces of the tape to the bottom of shoe. Make sure the tape is securely placed so that it isn't noticeable from a distance.

Quarters. If you live in a windy city such as Chicago, you might be a little reluctant to wear fuller, lighter-weight skirts for fear of showing your "goods" to the entire city. Stylists tape quarters or fishing weights to the inside seam of the skirt to help weigh it down and prevent it from flying up.

Polaroid or digital camera. Stylists use these cameras to help keep track of their outfits. For example, if a certain outfit looks fabulous on you, take a picture of yourself wearing it so that you will remember what you wore. If you have a lot of shoes, you can also paste a Polaroid on the outside of each shoebox to help identify your shoes.

Deodorant stain removers. After I gave several great shirts away to Goodwill because of deodorant stains, a stylist friend of mine told me about deodorant stain removal pads. These pads remove the white chalk deodorant stains from dark-colored garments with relative ease. They are available online and at department stores.

Organizing Your Closet

Keeping an organized closet is another secret budget fashionista tool. It helps me easily identify gaps in my wardrobe, and it also stops me from purchasing redundant items. An easy step in organizing your closet is to place the most frequently worn items in the front and the less frequently used items in garment bags (with vents to breathe) in at the back of the closet. That way you don't have to dig through your closet to find items you frequently look for.

Make sure that you don't store your clothing in those plastic dry cleaner bags. They are designed for temporary protection of your clothes and don't allow your clothes to breathe. And, at the risk of sounding like Joan Crawford, wire hangers are *bad* for your clothes. They create unsightly creases on pants and at the shoulders of your shirts. Use either plastic or wooden hangers. (Padded hangers are fine, too, but are much more expensive.) Ikea has great wooden hangers for under $5 for a set of six, a great investment in keeping your clothes looking great.

Inside Scoop: *Robert Finney, Chief Operating Officer of Drylans Cleaners*

Owning a dry-cleaning business is one surefire way for budget fashionistas to save money on their cleaning bills. Lucky for me, my family owns a dry-cleaning business in Minneapolis, Minnesota, and my brother Robert is the family's dry-cleaning expert. As the chief operating officer of Drylans Cleaners (www.drylans.com), he is an encyclopedia of fabric care information. Schooled in the ways of the budget fashionista by his sister, Robert gives us the lowdown on how to save money on dry cleaning.

What Is Dry Cleaning?

It is important to understand the entire dry-cleaning process—from the time you bring in your garments to when you pick them up. Dry cleaning is anything but dry. In fact, it is a very wet process that involves a liquid solvent, the most common being perchloroethylene (also known as perc). Garments brought to the cleaners are placed in a receiving area. A good cleaner will read the care instructions (those funny little symbols) and check the garment for stains. Any stains will be treated with a variety of stain removal solvents. The clothes are then put in a really big machine, similar to a washing machine, that will clean them using perc, and dry them as well. So they go in dry and come out dry. Most people don't realize that their clothes are almost always washed with other folks' clothes. The perc is such a strong solvent, however, that it kills any nasty germs.

How Can a Budget Fashionista Save Money on Dry-Cleaning Bills?

One way that budget fashionistas can save money on cleaning bills is to stop overcleaning suits. Suits should be cleaned only once or twice a year. You can send your suit to the cleaners to get it pressed more often. Use a fabric-freshening product like Febreze to keep the clothing fresh between visits to the dry cleaner (test a nonvisible section of the garment to make sure it is color safe). You can also use a little

Febreze on the garment to reduce that just-from-the-cleaner smell. At-home dry-cleaning systems are good for touch-ups between dry-cleaning trips, but they don't clean as well and you still have to press the garment.

You can also save a ton of money by gently washing your cashmere sweaters at home. In fact, this prolongs the life of a sweater. First check to make sure the sweater doesn't have any special trim or embellishment that requires it to be dry-cleaned. If none are present, pour a small amount (about the size of a quarter) of baby shampoo into a clean sink filled with cool water. Swirl the sweater around in the sink for one to two minutes and then let it soak for ten minutes. Drain the sink and gently rinse and squeeze the garment until all the soap is gone. Once the soap is gone, carefully squeeze the water out of the garment and lay it flat on a towel. Use another towel (you might need two) to soak up the excess water. Shape the sweater and let it lie flat to dry.

Budget Fashionista Tip #11: Make a Closet Sachet

A closet sachet is a great way to keep your clothes smelling fresh, especially during the humid summer months, and is fairly easy to make. The first step is to cut a 4-by-8-inch strip of cloth from an old T-shirt or bedsheet. Fold the cloth over so that it is 4 by 4 inches. Stitch the sides of the cloth, leaving an opening at the top. Add your favorite potpourri, some rose petals, a few pine needles, or scented crystals until the sachet is approximately three-fourths full. Stitch the top of the sachet closed using needle and thread. Add a string to hang in the closet or place it in a drawer. You can also place several cedar chips in an old mesh produce bag and hang it in your closet. You can get the same effect by hanging a scented dryer sheet on a hook in your closet. Dryer sheets also work well as scented liners for your dresser drawers and for deodorizing smelly shoes.

See "The Budget Fashionista's Mini-Guide to Taking Care of Clothes" (page 221) for more clothing care information.

Chapter 6

Clumpy, Frumpy, and Lumpy: The Importance of Good Undergarments

If your undergarments are stretched, stained, bleached out, discolored, or otherwise abused, throw them out—NOW.

Just as a painter must properly prepare his or her canvas, a budget fashionista must properly prepare her canvas—in this case, her body. Wearing the correct bra and panties can have a huge impact on how your clothes hang on your body, making you look and feel slimmer. After all, what's the point of wearing a hot Nicole Miller dress if your butt looks like a carton of Chunky Monkey ice cream? It doesn't matter if you scored a great pair of pants at the Chaiken sample sale if your Hanes Her Way have lost their direction.

Don't underestimate the importance of proper undergarments; they transform not only your outer self but your inner self as well. I once received an e-mail from Kasey, a reader who worked at a very large bank and who often felt overlooked by her mostly male coworkers in their weekly office meetings. She had read one of my blog entries where I discussed how budget fashionistas could use sexy lingerie to bring a little personality into a wardrobe dominated by corporate suits. Kasey took this tip a step further and purchased two Wonder Woman camisole and panty sets to wear under her boring black suits. Every time she wore one of the sets, she felt empowered by the fact that she was in on an inside joke. In her e-mail she elaborated on how she imagined tying the office bigmouth to his chair with her invisible rope when he interrupted her during meetings and discussions. Kasey was promoted to vice president within six months.

Fashionable Flashback: My Boob Saga

I wore the wrong bra size for years. Like many women, I bought bras as an afterthought—sort of like remembering to floss after brushing. In fact, I didn't get a proper-fitting bra until I was twenty-two years old—eleven years after my first training bra. Appalled by the sad state of my breasts (I wore sports bras that made me look as if I had a uniboob), my mother and grandmother marched me straight to Saks Fifth Avenue and got me fitted by a wonderful woman named Antonia. My breasts have never been the same since.

So profound was this interaction with Antonia that I started a crusade to make sure all my friends (including you) learn the importance of proper-fitting undergarments. Antonia rocked my undergarment world when she taught me such tips as how the middle section of the bra should lie flat against your breastbone, and if you're over a C cup, underwire is your best friend. She turned me into a bra crusader, leading me to call up my friends' mothers (moms and grandmas are very big on underwear; it's as if giving birth somehow increases their attachment to undergarments) to enlist their help in ensuring that their loved ones have adequate support.

Bra Myths Dispelled

Increasing your band size will compensate for a smaller cup size. False. Although increasing from a 36 to a 38 will slightly increase the width of the cup, it doesn't increase the volume of the cup.

Tighten your shoulder strap for support. Shoulder straps are there for additional guidance, not for primary support. If you have a proper-fitting bra, your breasts will still be in place and supported with or without straps.

You need to get fitted for a bra only once in your lifetime. Your breasts, like your body, change over time. Since getting fitted is free and budget fashionistas like free services, you should get fitted at least once a year.

Sports bras are great everyday bras. Sports bras may be more comfortable than traditional underwire bras, but there's nothing cute about a "uniboob."

The Budget Fashionista Explains: How to Figure Out Your Bra Size

Your bra size is determined by measuring your body at two different points.

First there is the **band measurement.** Use a soft measuring tape to measure around your rib cage, directly under your breasts. Add three inches to this number. This is your band measurement, the number in your bra size (for example, the **36** in 36C). If your band measurement is an odd number, add another inch to get your size.

Then there is the **bust measurement.** Wearing your best bra, measure loosely around the fullest part of your bust. Subtract your band measurement from this measurement, and find the resulting number in the chart on the next page. This will tell your cup size (for example: the **C** in 36C).

Building a Bra Wardrobe

You need to build an underwear wardrobe as much as you need to build a clothing wardrobe. Every budget fashionista should have the following bras in her lingerie drawer:

Black bra:	the foundation of the foundation that can pretty much be worn with anything
Flesh-colored bra:	great for wearing underneath lighter-colored garments

Cup Size Chart	
Difference in Inches Between Band and Bust Measurements	Cup Size
1	A
2	B
3	C
4	D
5	DD
6	DDD/E
7	DDDD
8	F
9	G
10	H

Strapless bra: perfect for strapless and spaghetti-strapped tops and tank tops

Sports bra: keeps "the girls" well supported when working out

Weekend bra: so comfortable you could sleep in it; also look for undershirts with a built-in bra shelf

T-shirt bra: gives you a smooth layer underneath T-shirts and thin clingy tops

Sexy demi bra: not every bra has to be practical

Major support bra: a bra that would make your grandmother proud; look for those with underwire and thick straps

Take a look inside your lingerie drawer. Using the form on the next page, indicate whether you have the following basic bras:

Bra Inventory Form		
Type of Bra	**Yes**	**No**
Black		
Flesh-colored		
Strapless		
Sports		
Weekend		
T-shirt		
Sexy demi		
Major support		

Upon completing the above form, you'll probably notice that you have some gaps in your bra wardrobe. For these basics I suggest going to old-school staple stores like JC Penney, Macy's, Saks Fifth Avenue, and, yes, even Sears. These stores have trained people who can measure you and place you in bras for free. These women are skilled at the art of support, and there is no obligation to buy. I suggest that you find the most senior (read oldest) member of the lingerie staff to measure you. Most likely she has seen many a boob in her day, so let the woman do her job. I once witnessed a fellow customer, who obviously had no concept of Reality Dressing, yell at a trained bra specialist because she suggested a larger bra size. Yes, you were a 34B in high school, but like feathered hair, that time has passed.

If you feel guilty, like me, buy one bra from the shop after getting measured, sort of like a thank-you for the service, and then at home visit a site like Figleaves.com to find the same bras cheaper. These sites always have discounts and almost always offer free shipping and other discount codes through thebudgetfashionista.com.

Remember, you don't wear the same size in every bra. Bras by European lingerie companies (La Perla, Cosabella, and Chantelle) tend to run smaller than bras manufactured by American companies (Playtex, Olga, and Wacoal).

Budget Fashionista Tip #12: Caring for Your Unmentionables

DON'T THROW YOUR BRAS IN THE DRYER. Yes, it's easier, but the dryer causes the elastic to stretch, thus reducing the life span of the bra. Wash bras and delicate items in a sink using lukewarm water and baby laundry soap or baby shampoo. If you must use a washing machine, place your bras and underwear in a mesh lingerie bag, found at most dollar stores. Always hang your fine undergarments on a rack or clothesline to dry.

The Budget Fashionista Guide to Bras

Type of Top	Type of Bra	Brands
Plunging neckline	Push-up or plunge	Wonderbra, Felina, Lily of France
T-shirt	Seamless T-shirt	Jockey, Wacoal, Warner's
Backless shirt	Adhesive cups	Fashion Forms
White or light-colored	A shade close to your skin color	La Perla Black collection, Olga
Strapless	Strapless	Wacoal, Wonderbra
Sheer or see-through	Adhesive cups	Fashion Forms
Cropped	Great support	Wacoal, Rigby, and Peller

Now for the Panties

I thought it was common knowledge that underpant sizes don't correspond directly with clothing sizes, just as shoe sizes don't correspond directly with the length of your foot. Unfortunately, some fashionistas never learned this important fashion lesson.

My friend Carla* is one of those fashionistas. Carla is a brilliant, beautiful techie who builds Microsoft Access databases for fun. Out of the blue one day over lunch she told me she had a pair of underwear for me. Although I love Carla, I thought her partner, Rob, might think it was weird that she bought underwear for another woman. Apparently Carla, who wears a size 6 to 8 in clothes, thought that underpant sizes matched clothing sizes. In a moment of desperation that can only be brought on by the early arrival of a woman's monthly visitor Carla purchased a package of size 9 cotton panties. She was now stuck with a pair of bloomers that were way too big for her and wanted to pass them on to her friend with the biggest butt.

Never one to pass up a freebie, I gladly took the bloomers. I had to wash them three times to shrink them and while drying them for the third time, I drew up this chart for my dear friend Carla and other fashionistas who are confused about the sizing system for panties.

Panty Size Chart		
Panty Size	**Pants Size**	**Corresponding Size**
4	0–4	XS
5	4–8	S
6	8–12	M
7	12–16	L
8	16–20	XL
9	20–24	XXL
10	24–28	XXXL

* Name changed to protect the innocent.

The Budget Fashionista Explains:
To Wear Pantyhose or Not Wear Pantyhose?

There's a raging debate in the dressing rooms of the world regarding pantyhose. Some fashionistas think that it's a major faux pas to wear pantyhose, while others think it is a major faux pas not to. Use common sense to answer this question. If it's 100 degrees outside, it's pretty stupid to wear pantyhose; however, if it's 20 degrees outside, it's stupid not to wear pantyhose. Also, if you work in certain conservative office environments, wearing pantyhose is a requirement. (Of course, in some environments, like the fashion industry, anything goes, but when it's cold, keep those legs covered.)

Best Budget-Friendly Places to Buy Lingerie

Bare Necessities (www.barenecessities.com). View their bra and panty guides for detailed information and tips on finding the perfect undergarments. They also have a pretty amazing selection of bras for every size.

Daffy's (www.daffys.com). Based in the Northeast, this is one of my favorite places to shop for lingerie. I once purchased three Donna Karan sports bras (retail price $50) for $14.95 apiece.

Figleaves (www.figleaves.com). One of the biggest online lingerie stores in the U.K., it now has a U.S.–based site. They have a huge selection of designer undergarments, sleepwear, and swimwear from Dolce & Gabbana, La Perla, Chantelle, and more. They also have great online coupons.

Frederick's of Hollywood (www.fredericksofHollywood.com). Invoking the spirit of Hollywood glamour, this store will take you from broken bust to bombshell with their affordable sexy lingerie.

H&M (www.hm.com). This clothing chain, known for its designer-inspired fashions, also carries bras, panties, nightgowns, and hosiery inspired by the likes of La Perla for well under $30.

Jockey (www.jockey.com). Their incredibly comfortable line of cotton underwear makes Jockey an excellent stop for the anti-underwire crowd.

Off 5th, Saks Fifth Avenue Outlet. Get measured at the main Saks but head to the outlet store to purchase expensive bras from high-end lingerie companies like Lejaby and Rigby Peller, for up to 80 percent off their original price. The bra section can be difficult to find at the outlet store. It's usually located in an obscure corner near the ladies' fitting rooms.

Sears (www.sears.com). Sears has supplied generations of women with their no-nonsense but extremely supportive bras. A great stop for basic bras under $30.

Target (www.target.com). While it has one of the biggest and best everyday underwear departments in the country, it unfortunately doesn't have a fit specialist on hand. I love its hip, affordable sleepwear sets from Swell by Cynthia Rowley and Fred Said.

T.J. Maxx (www.tjmaxx.com). This discount retailer has a huge selection of designer bras and undergarments straight from your favorite department stores. Find favorites like Nancy Ganz bodyshapers and Natori sleepwear.

Victoria's Secret (www.victoriassecret.com). This lingerie store, with its popular catalog and online site, is a favorite of mall dwellers and teenage boys. Although I wouldn't necessarily suggest this store for support bras, it is a great place for sexy bras and lingerie.

Wal-Mart (www.walmart.com). As a stylist I've been known to use the thongs from Wal-Mart in my shoots because models frequently forget to bring the correct undergarments. They look exactly like D&G thongs, and they cost $1.99.

Chapter 7

Accessory Power

As of the writing of this book, I have approximately 36 pairs of earrings, 28 necklaces, 21 handbags, 16 pairs of shoes, 11 scarves, 10 belts, 8 brooches, 5 watches, 3 hat pins, and a wedding ring. I love accessories.

As a rule of thumb you should spend about one-third of your shopping budget on accessories. This amount may be adjusted up or down, depending on your accessory needs. Before you head out to the nearest Claire's, there are a few rules you must observe for wearing accessories:

1. **Put it where you want people to look.** Eyes will be drawn to where you place the accessory, so if you are not very fond of your earlobes, you might not want to wear a pair of chandelier earrings. For items like a great bag, pay attention to where the purse falls, because that will accent the area. I have a big butt, so I try not to carry bags that fall right at my hip area. If you have a few extra pounds around your middle, you don't want to carry a bag that hits right at your waist. Try a purse that hits higher or lower. Be sure that the purse is in scale with your body. If you are a larger size, a small bag will make you look larger than a bigger bag.

2. **Choose one primary accessory and build around it.** Pick an accessory to be the focal point of the outfit. As fashionistas we love to pile on the jewelry, which is great, but just make sure it is all going in a similar direction or fits into the overall look. Too much bling is not a good thing.

3. **Check the quality.** Wearing costume (fake) jewelry is totally acceptable and even encouraged for budget fashionistas. Wearing green metal or heavily tarnished metal, however, is not acceptable. If the gold plate has started to flake off your necklace, throw it out.

I like accessories because they're much cheaper than a new suit, and you can get a lot for less money. They're more durable than a pair

Expensive vs. Budget: Accessories by Personal Style Type		
Personal Style	**Expensive ($50+)**	**Budget (Less Than $50)**
Sporty	Coach, Lily Pulitzer, Le Sport Sac, Longchamp, Dooney & Burke, J. Crew	Nine West, Aerosoles, Old Navy, Tommy Hilfiger, the Gap
Trendy	Roberto Cavalli, Dolce & Gabbana, BCBG Max Azria, L.A.M.B.	Victoria's Secret, Forever 21, Torrid, Claire's, Charlotte Russe
Conservative	Salvatore Ferragamo, Stuart Weitzman, St. John, Tiffany, Brighton, Calvin Klein	Talbots, Lord & Taylor brand, Nordstrom brand, Keds, Ann Taylor, Liz Claiborne
Socialite	Chanel, Gucci, Prada, Judith Ripka, Harry Winston, Cartier, Giuseppe Zanotti	Monet, Carolee, Banana Republic, New York & Company, Club Monaco
Urban Trekker	Kenneth Cole, Donna Karan, Balenciaga, Marc Jacobs	Dollhouse, Rampage, Brass Plum, Necessary Objects
Romantic	Tracy Reese, Nanette Lepore, Kate Spade, Sigrid Olsen, My Flat in London, Lulu Guinness, Hollywould	Newport News, Franco Sarto, Kathy handbags and accessories, LaRedoute.com

of jeans, so you can (and should) keep them forever. Moreover, almost every store on the planet has an accessories department—from the ultra ritzy Bergdorf Goodman to H&M to the local Goodwill.

The Budget Fashionista Explains:
Developing Your Signature Piece

In this time of mass consumption and instant access, there exists very little originality, especially in the area of personal style. Thus, the development of a signature piece—an item or style that will help identify you as unique, sort of like a fashion "calling card"—becomes increasingly important. Your signature piece can be great shoes (Missy Elliott), a haircut (Jennifer Aniston, Halle Berry), or great dresses (Hilary Swank)—anything that adds originality to your look. It's okay to splurge on these pieces because they are items that help you define and enhance your style. Focus on building a wardrobe of these signature pieces.

You don't have to be a celebrity stylist to find your signature item. Review your charts from Chapter 5. Is there a particular clothing item or accessory that dominates your closet? If so, develop that piece into your signature item. If there is no piece that dominates your closet, think of the item of clothing you wear the most and develop this item into your signature piece.

Choose a signature piece that reflects your personality and your lifestyle, and that you can maintain on your budget. (My signature pieces are accessories, particularly earrings, because I can purchase great accessories for reasonable prices.) If you work in an entry-level position, you shouldn't choose diamonds as your signature accessory, but great purses is an affordable option. Make these pieces so fabulous that it won't matter if the rest of your outfit came from Goodwill.

Budget Fashionista Tip #13: Outline with Expensive and Color In with Cheap

If you feel the need to splurge, you'll get more bang for your buck by purchasing a purse and a great pair of shoes (not necessarily at the same time) from a well-known, high-end designer such as Gucci, Chanel, Yves Saint Laurent (YSL), Fendi, Hogan, Bottega Veneta, or Balenciaga. Frame yourself with these expensive items, and it really won't matter how much everything in between costs. Even if you are dressed down to your skivvies in Goodwill, everyone will assume your outfit is expensive because of your expensive accessories.

Purses: My Favorite Accessory

I love handbags. I *really* love handbags. Case in point:

Fashionable Flashback

One day while shopping in New York City, I was on a mission to find the perfect tote bag and somehow ended up on Fifth Avenue. For those who have never been to the Big Apple, Fifth Avenue is home to some of the most exclusive luxury stores in the world, including the don of bling, Harry Winston, überfabulous Bergdorf Goodman, and the flagship store of Saks Fifth Avenue. On a strict budget, I had no business browsing in the Cole Haan store on this famous avenue, but I was lured into the store by a tote bag staring longingly at me from the display window. The bag, which cost more than my car note, was simply beautiful—the color of Ben & Jerry's caramel sundae topping, and with a silver circular clasp. I wanted it more than I wanted a fake ID in college.

As *budget fashionistas we've all wanted a great item or piece that we couldn't really afford. Most of us turn away from the purchase, which is exactly what I should have done. Despite my budget constraints, I bought the bag and a matching small handbag (which I later sold on eBay).*

I love purses because they can instantly identify your personality and be used to "fake" your income level. For example, if you're carrying a $1,000 Christian Dior bag, it doesn't matter if you're wearing a jogging suit from Kmart—people will assume you're wealthy because of the bag. The folks who sell knockoffs understand this point all too well. In order for this to work, choose a status bag that doesn't have its logos plastered all over it. Trust me, carrying those types of bags makes you look as if you're trying too hard to look "wealthy." Designers such as Hermès, Celine, Marc Jacobs, Tods, Balenciaga, Mulberry, and Luella all have great bags that scream "Look at me, I'm rich" with the right amount of tact. If you are broke, then search for inspired versions of these bags from Kathy Van Zeeland, Hype, BCBG Max Azria, Kenneth Cole, and Nine West.

Great Stores and Websites for Designer and Designer-Inspired Bags

Ashford (www.ashford.com). This designer superstore has a wide selection of designer purses—from Prada to Gucci to Lulu Guinness—for up to 80 percent off the retail price.

Bluefly (www.bluefly.com). This online retailer has a large assortment of designer bags from Marc Jacobs, Anya Hindmarch, Fendi, Ferragamo, and more, for up to 65 percent off. They usually don't stock many of these bags, so when you see one, you need to buy it ASAP.

Century 21 (www.c21store.com). This mega designer discount store is a favorite of East Coast fashionistas. The lower-Manhattan location has a huge (and messy) purse section with bags from companies like XOXO, Hype, Dolce & Gabbana, and Judith Leiber for up to 80 percent off the retail price. Avoid the store on weekends and during lunchtime.

Inside Scoop: Elissa Bloom, Accessory Designer and Global Fashionista

New York–based accessory designer Elissa Bloom (www.elissabloom .com) knows good bags. Her eponymous accessory collection has developed a huge following and is sold at Bloomingdale's, Fred Segal, Takashimaya, Nordstrom, and Verve, as well as in countless other upscale boutiques throughout the United States. This international fashionista gives her thoughts on what to look for when shopping for accessories.

Why are accessories important?

Accessories make the woman, and I feel they are the one thing that sets her apart and gives her a unique identity. Clothing these days seems to be so standard and repetitive; accessories should be the main focus of attention on a woman. I suggest investing in one great quality bag or piece of jewelry that you absolutely love—one that is ageless and functional. I always ask myself the following questions before purchasing higher priced accessories: Do I absolutely love this? Is this something I can see myself wearing three years from now? What makes this special and unique? What are the different outfits I can make or ways I can wear this item?

What should a budget fashionista look for when shopping for accessories?

Look for functionality when buying accessories. Function is so important. That's why I design my bags with lots of pockets—for easy access to keys and ringing cell phones. I can tell a good quality accessory by the materials used. Is it cheap material that is going to rip after a few wears, or is it quality material? (You can always tell by the feel of the fabric.) Also, notice the hardware of the bag and how it is finished— the stitching, zipper pulls, snaps, and straps reveal a lot about the quality of the item. For example, are the straps reinforced?

Charlotte Russe (www.charlotterusse.com). This is another one of my favorite stores. It doesn't get as much hype as its competitor For- ever 21, but its accessory and shoe departments are equally good. The shoe selection is very trend-centered, so don't expect to find good walking shoes, but the belt and purse selections are first-rate.

Forzieri (www.forzieri.com). Based in Florence, Italy, this online shop has an impressive selection of leather goods, fine jewelry, and stylish apparel. Prices on the main site can be pretty steep, so click on the outlet section for exclusive deals on the best in Italian fashion.

H&M (www.hm.com). H&M is the Ikea of clothing stores. Their accessory selection depends on location. Most mall-based stores aren't as well stocked as flagship stores, but they still offer a great se- lection of trendy necklaces and are *the* store for cheap earrings, with prices starting at $1.90 for classic goldtone hoops.

Loehmann's@SmartBargains (www.smartbargains.com). Loeh- mann's and the discount website Smart Bargains joined together to put Loehmann's amazing selection of designer goods online as the joint venture Loehmann's@SmartBargains. You'll find a huge selec- tion of designer bags from Gucci, Tods, Prada, and more, for up to 80 percent off retail prices.

Off 5th, Saks Fifth Avenue Outlet. This is hands down my favorite outlet store. Its impressive selection of heavily discounted designer purses from heavy hitters like Fendi, Furla, Longchamp, Kate Spade, and Juicy Couture gives broke fashionistas like myself the perfect pieces to outline our outfits.

Rodeo Drive Resale (www.rodeodriveresale.com). A favorite of West Coast fashion insiders, this consignment/resale boutique has a great selection of new and consigned designer bags from St. John to Chanel, all for prices you can actually afford.

Sears (www.sears.com). Yes, Sears. Skip the appliances and head right to the accessories department (usually located across the aisle from the juniors section), where you'll find an impressive selection of accessories, shoes, and other items at very budget-friendly prices. Focus on purchasing pieces that look expensive (not gaudy). My fashionable friends fawn over my silver beaded 1920s-style handbag. Little do they know (well, at least until now) that I bought it at the Sears at the Mall of America in Minnesota.

Strawberry. This East Coast–based store has one of the largest selections of designer-inspired purses for well under $20. I once purchased a Pucci-like flower canvas duffle—exactly like the one carried by Carrie in *Sex and the City*—for $9.99. The jewelry department isn't too shabby, either. Unfortunately, the store doesn't have a website.

T.J. Maxx (www.tjmaxx.com). This national discount store carries designer bags from Ralph Lauren, Hype, and Coach. My best purchase from T.J. Maxx was a small cream-colored Coach saddlebag at the store in Philadelphia for $49.99 (retail price $119.99). Make sure to visit their online superstore.

Visit TheBudgetFashionista.com for a complete listing of great stores for bags and purses.

Earrings, Necklaces, and Bracelets

Earrings, necklaces, and bracelets are perhaps the most cost-effective accessories. Hit a store during a great sale, and you can stock up on several pairs of earrings for less than $10. When shopping for earrings, it's important to choose a pair that works with your facial shape. To accentuate your facial features, focus on wearing jewelry that mimics the shape of those features (angular features/angular jewelry; curved features/curved jewelry). To balance your features, focus on wearing jewelry that is the opposite (angular features/curved jewelry; curved features/angular jewelry).

Budget Fashionista Tip #14: Lost an Earring? Here's What to Do with the One Left

• Use vintage post or clip earrings in place of brooches as lapel pins.

• If the earring is made of a precious metal (silver, gold, or platinum), take it to a jeweler and see if the missing earring can be re-created or if you can sell the metal to the jeweler.

• If the earring is large enough, take it to a jeweler and see if it can be turned into a ring or pendant.

Great Places for Jewelry

Claire's Boutique (www.claires.com). Although most of the items are made for the junior high set, the store carries inspired versions of the latest trends for well under $20. Also visit their sister store, Icing.

Forever 21 (www.forever21.com). Whether you're twenty-one or eighty-one, it's worth visiting this store's accessory section. I suggest shopping in the morning on a weekday or early Saturday morning to avoid the after-school crowds.

Fred Flare (www.fredflare.com). This is a great site for those who want a little more edge to their accessories. Hipsters head here to find everything from earrings shaped like guitars to the affordable bling of the Loop bags.

ICE (www.ice.com). This site was created with budget fashionistas in mind. It features quality diamonds and gemstones in stylish settings at prices you can afford.

Laila Rowe (www.lailarowe.com). This store is an accessory lover's dream. Most of their gypsy-influenced earrings, necklaces, bags, and scarves retail for well under $30.

Lord & Taylor (www.lordandtaylor.com). Known mostly for inexpensive but high-quality cashmere sweaters, Lord & Taylor also has a rather large accessory department. Head to their website for special in-store coupons.

Target (www.target.com). Target has an amazing selection of earrings from their Xhilaration line, as well as a bridge line from the mega costume jewelry manufacturer Monet. Their jewelry section is usually located at the front of the store, near their impressive selection of bags.

Thrift stores and garage sales. Thrift stores and garage sales are the next best thing to raiding Grandma's closets. There is no better place to find quality vintage jewelry for less. My favorite necklace, a turquoise rope necklace, I purchased from the Salvation Army for 25 cents. When you buy earrings, make sure you clean the posts with rubbing alcohol or hydrogen peroxide before wearing.

Urban Outfitters (www.urbanoutfitters.com). Urban Trekkers love this store for its boho styled jewelry and accessories. It also has an amazing selection of vintage-like bags and shoes.

Wal-Mart (www.walmart.com). Believe or not, Wal-Mart has an excellent selection of designer-inspired pieces for ridiculously low prices. I found a sterling silver heart link bracelet, similar to a version sold at the high-end jewelry store Tiffany, for less than $20. Only you and the cashier will know you bought it from Wal-Mart.

Visit TheBudgetFashionista.com for a complete listing of great stores for jewelry.

Shoes, Glorious Shoes

If bags are my first love, then shoes run a close second. Shoes are one of the most important elements of your wardrobe. They are often the first thing people notice about your personal appearance. Shoes also have the power to completely change the look of an outfit. For example, a pair of heels instantly dresses up a pair of jeans, while a pair of sneakers instantly makes the jeans more casual. And wearing a pair of knee-high, three-inch-heeled boots gives a basic black dress a more fashionable vibe than a simple pair of black flats.

DEAR DSW:

From the moment I first stepped into your store, I knew I was in love. I'm getting misty-eyed just talking about you. I was a bit reluctant to enter into a relationship with you at first, since I was just coming out of a shaky long-term relationship with another Budget Fashionista favorite, Nordstrom's Rack. However, you turned out to be more than a store: You became my best friend and a shoulder to cry on when I felt that all was lost for my size 11 feet. At least once a week, I walk down shoe-after-shoe-filled aisle, swooning over your selection of shoes from the likes of Christian Dior, Nicole Miller, Jimmy Choo, Coach, Roberto Cavalli, Burberry, Sesto Meccui, Via Spiga, Kate Spade, BCBG, and more for up to 80 percent off the retail price.

My strategy when visiting your store is to head to your clearance section, which is usually located in the back. I've been known to block off the entire size 10 and up rack like a mother tiger protecting her baby cubs. I almost fainted when I found a pair of cream-colored Kate Spade flat sandals in a size 11 for $13.98. I cried tears of joy when I found a pair of white satin strappy sandals by Kenneth Cole for my wedding for $9.98. I was crowned Queen of DSW when I purchased eleven pairs of shoes for $120 in your store in St. Louis Park, Minnesota.

You have truly changed my life, and on behalf of all budget fashionistas, I thank you.

With love,

The Budget Fashionista

The Budget Fashionista Explains:
The European Shoe Size Chart

European designers often use a sizing system that is different from that of American designers, and it can be pretty confusing for shoppers. Below is a standard size-conversion chart, though generally, when trying on shoes, make sure you try a half size up and a half size down to get a good fit. European shoes tend to fit about a half size smaller than their corresponding American size.

Women's International Shoe Size Chart										
American										
6	6.5	7	7.5	8	8.5	9	9.5	10	10.5	11/11.5
European										
36/36.5	37	37.5	38	38.5/39	39.5	40	40.5	41	41.5	42
United Kingdom										
3.5	4	4.5	5	5.5	6	6.5	7	7.5	8	8/8.5

Great Places for Shoes

dELiA*S (www.delias.com). Although this store is known mostly for its casual teen wear, their shoe selection is the perfect source for trendy shoes for budget fashionistas of any age. Head to the site and find designer-inspired versions of the latest styles, in sizes up to 11, for up to 75 percent less than the price of the designer versions.

DSW (www.dswshoewarehouse.com). My favorite shoe store. This store carries many size 11 shoes, which is great for big-footed fashionistas like myself. Make sure you sign up for their rewards club that frequently sends out discount coupons and rewards for every $250 you spend.

Last Call Neiman Marcus (www.neimanmarcus.com). Budget fashionistas should skip the main store and head to the outlet, which has high-end designers at amazingly low prices. You'll find footwear from designers like Prada, Christian Louboutin, and Stuart Weitzman. Register in the store for their online newsletter to receive additional discounts.

Nordstrom Rack (www.nordstrom.com). This store houses the same shoes as the main store, but at significantly reduced prices and in sizes up to 13 in women's shoes and 16 in men's shoes. I once found a pair of brown Ferragamo one-inch-heel pumps for $45. The store also has a great children's shoe department. Sign up to receive notices of special shoe events.

Off 5th, Saks Fifth Avenue Outlet. You will find an enormous selection of high-end shoes from Ferragamo, Delman, Beverly Feldman, Gucci, Manolo Blahnik, Marc Jacobs, Tods, and Ralph Lauren Purple Label from size 5 to 11. Make sure you sign up for their mailing list to get coupons and invitations to special events.

Old Navy (www.oldnavy.com). Old Navy has firmly cornered the flip-flop market. They actually made the plastic sandals you used to buy at Walgreens stylish and affordable. All you need is $10 to fund your entire summer sandal wardrobe.

Payless (www.payless.com). Okay, you can stop laughing. I'm not suggesting that you hook up with a pair of pleather shoes, but definitely look in the store for sandals (they carry the cutest espadrilles) and simple canvas shoes. The Starlet line by Star Jones, worn by her celebrity bridesmaids Natalie Cole, Vivica Fox, and Karena Gore Schiff, has hot evening sandals for well under $30. This low-priced shoe store continues to be the best place to find dyeable shoes.

Shoebuy (www.shoebuy.com). This is another great online shoe store that offers free shipping, free returns, and 110 percent price guarantees. I usually compare Shoebuy prices to the prices of Zappos.com.

Target (www.target.com). Everyone raves about the Isaac Mizrahi for Target collection; however, I'm a big fan of the trendy Mossimo line. Target is also a wonderful place to find "designer-inspired" versions of hot shoe trends such as stilettos and suede boots.

Zappos (www.zappos.com). This is the biggest shoe store on the Web. Searching through the site can be a bit daunting, but their huge selection of women's, men's, and children's shoes from Emilio Pucci to Keds guarantees that you will find something to fit your budget. Plus, someone was smart enough to offer both free shipping and free returns.

Visit TheBudgetFashionista.com for a complete listing of great stores for jewelry, shoes, and other accessories.

Transforming Your Outfits with Accessories

Budget Fashionista Tip #15: Go E.L.F.

To go quickly from drab worker bee to sexy vixen on a budget, remember E.L.F. (ears, lips, and feet). Wear bold chandelier earrings, bold lipstick (L'Oréal cherry is my favorite), and bold shoes (Manolos or Steve Madden) to transform your corporate blues to nighttime fashion.

Below are some examples of how you can use accessories to transform an outfit.

Your situation: You work in the financial industry, and your closet is filled with nice conservative black business suits. You've been invited on a hot date after work and want to look like a million bucks. Your first instinct is to head to the nearest mall on your lunch break and purchase a completely new outfit.

BUDGET FASHIONISTA SOLUTION: Step back from the department store. Head to your nearest Target. Purchase a pair of sexy heels from Isaac Mizrahi and a pair of gold chandelier earrings from Swell by Cynthia Rowley. Sexy, simple, and under $30.

Your situation: You're invited to one of those beach or pool parties where the focus is on mingling, not swimming. You're excited about the party, but the idea of parading around in your swimsuit brings back horrible memories of sixth grade gym class.

BUDGET FASHIONISTA SOLUTION: Forget about gym class and channel the tropics. Go to your nearest Ross department store or Wal-Mart and purchase a pair of Jackie O. sunglasses, beaded thong sandals, simple pareo wrap, solid color one-piece swimsuit, and a beaded ponytail holder to create that "just-back-from-Saint-Tropez" look.

Your situation: Your husband's company is having their annual holiday party, and all you have is a basic black dress. Your husband is up for a big promotion, and you don't want him to be passed over because of the poor fashion sense of his wife.

BUDGET FASHIONISTA SOLUTION: Dust off that black dress. Impress the higher-ups by accessorizing with the highest possible heels you can walk in (falling will diminish the effect), fake diamond studs, and a pashmina wrap.

Chapter 8

Beauty 101

*E*very woman I know has an obsession with beauty products, whether publicly or secretly. This makes sense, because beauty products are the most affordable personal style tools. In this chapter you'll learn how to be a budget-conscious beauty junkie by devoting your beauty dollars to important beauty products (like foundation), conserving your dollars on products that can be bought for less (mascara), and creating your own home spa using what's in your fridge. You will be whipping up a temporary face-lift, making your own lip gloss, and shopping online at stores like Beauty.com faster than you can say "exfoliate."

My obsession with beauty products began when I was a child. My mother and I would hold "beauty nights," whipping up hair and facial masks from whatever was in the fridge. This obsession continued into adulthood with my addiction to all things MAC. At one point I had over twenty-one MAC eye shadows—most of which I never touched. I bought so many products from the MAC counter at Saks Fifth Avenue that I probably could have opened a MAC store in my bathroom.

What Is in My Beauty Drawer?

Oil of Olay Facial Moisturizer. *InStyle* and *Allure* magazines agree that this old standard continues to be one of the best facial moisturizers at any price. It softens and protects dry skin without the oily residue, and can be picked up from a local drugstore like CVS or Walgreens.

Dove Exfoliating Moisturizer Bar. In the wintertime my skin becomes extremely dry. Dove moisturizing soap is an inexpensive alternative to high-cost body washes, and it smells great.

Maybelline Great Lash Mascara. There is no reason to spend $20 on mascara when this makeup artist favorite can be found in local drugstores for less than $5.

Baby Vaseline. Nothing attacks crusty heels and dry winter skin like Vaseline. Yes, it is thick and somewhat messy. I suggest buying the baby version, which is softer and has a great baby powder scent.

Vitamin E capsules. The liquid version of the vitamin is a great treatment for bringing shine to your hair. You can also rub it on dry cuticles to soften and nourish nails.

Eyelash curler. Use this when you don't want to mess with fake eyelashes. It takes a while to get used to using this tool, but once you do, you won't ever leave your house without using it.

Tweezerman tweezers. Unless you are trying to channel the spirit of Frida Kahlo, these tweezers keep unruly eyebrows in top shape. I use my Tweezerman to get my eyebrows groomed between waxing.

Fake eyelashes. Nothing can change a look like a pair of fake eyelashes. Revlon makes great lashes with self adhesive so you can avoid the mess of eyelash glue.

What most beauty companies don't want you to know is that the best beauty product in the world is completely free: water—yep, good old H_2O. It clears your skin by helping to flush toxins from your system, and it helps support your vital organs. This is going to sound like a broken record, but you should drink at least eight glasses a day. Think of it this way: It's a whole lot cheaper and less painful than a face-lift.

Zits Happen: Quick Beauty Fixes from Your Fridge

Your refrigerator offers tons of quick beauty fixes without your having to spend a dime. Furthermore, your fridge can also be the source of your home spa, as explained later in this chapter. Here are several suggestions.

Bad breath	Baking soda works wonders for bad breath. Put a teaspoon on your toothbrush, add a little water, and brush as usual, including tongue and gums.
Blemishes	Squeeze juice from ½ lemon onto a cotton swab and sweep it over your face.
Cellulite	Warm dry coffee grounds and work them into your skin to help reduce cellulite.
Dry hair	In a pinch, use a little dab of skin lotion or Vaseline to moisturize your hair.
Dry skin	If no lotion is available, use hair conditioner. It works miracles in a pinch.
Dull hair	Be like the French and rinse your hair with a cup of champagne to brighten the hair color.
Dull skin	Dip a cotton ball in hydrogen peroxide and sweep it over skin as a toner. Be careful to avoid the eye area. You can also use vodka to spread on the skin.
Eyebrow tweezing and waxing pain	Apply a small amount of an oral topical anesthetic like Anbesol to help reduce the pain of tweezing and waxing.

Oily hair	A little baking soda sops the oil right up.
Puffy eyes	Put two cotton balls into ¼ cup of cold whole milk and place them on your eyes for five minutes.
Tired eyes	Steep two bags of green tea in a cup of water. Let cool (so you don't burn your eyelids) and place on closed eyes for fifteen minutes. You can also use chilled cucumbers.
Wet nails	Dip wet nails into ice-cold water for quick drying or spray with a cooking oil such as Pam. (I learned this from a nail technician.)
Wrinkles	Whip one egg and spread it on your face. Let it sit for fifteen minutes and then rinse thoroughly.

In my life as a fashion blogger and personal stylist, I've met quite a few makeup artists (called MUA in the industry). Being the nosy person that I am, I've always bugged them for tips and information on the different products they use as well as what is really worth the price and what is just packaging. An overwhelming majority of these MUAs say that you just need to spend money on foundation. For all the other products—lip gloss, nail polish, eye shadow, and mascara—there is little difference between drugstore brands and expensive department store brands.

Budget Fashionista Tip #16: Beware of Clearance Beauty Products

Be very careful when purchasing clearance beauty products. They may seem like a great deal, but they may be spoiled or expired. Always check the expiration dates on products.

Before heading out to your nearest Walgreens, I encourage you to visit Amazon.com and purchase *Making Faces* by Kevyn Aucoin. It will be the best $14 you've ever spent. A legend who died before his time, Aucoin was a makeup genius, transforming the looks of major stars such as Madonna, Mary J. Blige, Kate Moss,

Inside Scoop: *Celebrity Makeup Artist and Author Elke Von Freudenberg*

Elke Von Freudenberg reminds me of that really cool girl in high school—you know, the one who worked wonders in the girls' bathroom with a black eyeliner and a tub of Wet 'n' Wild lip gloss. All grown up, the former makeup queen of the high school bathroom (she received both her beauty school and high school diplomas on the same day) is now a highly sought after celebrity makeup artist and author of *The Makeup Course* eBook. Elke has worked her magic on celebrities as diverse as Kate Moss and Martin Short, and her polished and glamorous makeup style is often compared to the legendary makeup artist Kevyn Aucoin. A frequent contributing beauty editor, her work can be seen in such magazines as *Allure, Rolling Stone,* and *Paper.* During her brief break between the Oscars and Emmys, I got the celebrity makeup artist to dish some key beauty tips for budget fashionistas.

As a celebrity makeup artist, if you were shopping at your local Target or Wal-Mart, what products would you buy?

The Sonia Kashuk brand at Target stores is one of the best mass-market makeup lines around. It has good quality, color selection, and products that work. Two other great brands are Wet 'n' Wild, which has great lip and eye pencils and the best bronzer colors, and Revlon's Fabulash mascara, which is a close contender to Lancôme's famous mascaras.

What are some key beauty tips that budget fashionistas should know to look fabulous?

Apply blush first. If it looks great with nothing else on, you have the right amount on. Use a light brown eyebrow pencil as a lip pencil. It blends well with every lipstick you own. Nothing makes you look more dated or ages you faster than a thick foundation. Make sure your foundation blends into your skin. At the drugstore you sometimes only have three or four shades of concealer to choose from. Use your foundation to customize and create your perfect concealer by mixing a dot of your foundation into your concealer. Contrary to popular belief, you want your concealer to match your skin, not be two or three shades lighter.

Are there certain ingredients to look for when purchasing products that help determine whether or not it is a quality product?

Basically, all makeup product ingredients are the same. Quality is determined by how long the product will last. Always test blush and eye shadow colors on your fingers by applying a small amount to your hand and then rubbing it to test if it disappears quickly. If it comes off quickly, it will disappear just as fast on your face. To test foundations, apply a small amount to a sheet of white paper and observe whether or not an oil ring develops. If a ring does develop, the foundation may change color after you wear it for a short time. Also, check to see if the foundation looks too pink or gray on white paper. If it does, it will make your skin look fake or too ashy.

What are some of your favorite budget beauty products?

• Wet 'n' Wild medium bronzer (best color ever)

• Wet 'n' Wild lip gloss (just as glossy as MAC Lipglass)

• Revlon Fabulash (a brand-new favorite)

• e.l.f. eye shadows (less than $1). Their colors and staying power are fantastic.

and Tina Turner, and he influenced the makeup techniques of a generation of MUAs. This book will fundamentally change how you use makeup to enhance yourself and your image. Using beautifully illustrated pictures and real-life models, Aucoin teaches you how to make a great face step-by-step. He even includes tips for men.

Besides the great products recommended by Elke, here are some of my favorite budget beauty drugstore finds:

Baby wipes. Makeup artists use baby wipes to remove makeup. A fraction of the cost of the more expensive facial wipes, these wipes are equally as good.

Black Opal makeup stick. Finally, a great foundation for women of color. Fairer-skinned fashionistas will also love the foundation for the summer tan months.

Herbal Essence hair highlight system. It is simple to use, leaves your hair looking great, and is much cheaper than highlights at the salon.

Johnson's baby oil gel. Not as thick as Vaseline, this gel helps create nice, soft skin with a wonderful scent.

Pantene Pro-V shampoos and conditioners. Every major beauty and fashion publication has praised this line of beauty products. I love them because they calm my frizz-prone hair for well under $4.

Queen Helene conditioner. Even though it's found in the ethnic hair care section, fashionistas of all races swear by this conditioner. It strengthens and repairs hair for well under $5.

L'Oréal Colour Juice. There is no need to purchase the expensive Lancôme version when this lip gloss is excellent and well under $10.

Great Makeup Products at Any Price

Just as there is a car for every price range, there's also a lip gloss, mascara, and other makeup essentials. Use the following table to find the product that fits your budget.

You Want	Expensive (more than $10)	Budget (less than $10)
Juicy lip gloss	Lancôme	L'Oréal
Tinted moisturizer	Prescriptives	Neutrogena
Black mascara	Lancôme	Maybelline Great Lash
Self-tanning product	Lancôme	Bain de Soleil
Highlighter bronzing cream	Bobbi Brown	Wet 'n' Wild
Liquid eyeliner	NARS	Wet 'n' Wild
Great brushes	MAC brushes	Sonia Kashuk at Target
Eye shadow	NARS	Revlon
Conditioner for dry, damaged hair	Lancôme	Queen Helene
False eyelashes	MAC	Revlon
Everyday conditioner	Paul Mitchell	Herbal Essence
Moisture-rich lipstick	Chanel	L'Oréal

Budget Fashionista Tip #17: Sample Fragrances

If you are someone who wears perfume infrequently, then head to the nearest fragrance counter and request a free sample rather than purchase a full bottle. Most major fragrance companies, from Burberry to Kenzo, have samples of their products. Collect enough samples, and you will never have to purchase a bottle of perfume again.

Body and Skin Care on a Budget

Taking care of your body and skin is crucial to maintaining your status as a budget fashionista: You can't rock those Manolos that you

You Want	Expensive	Budget
Soft feet	Bliss Spa	Vaseline and thick white socks
Designer bath products	Barneys	Henri Bendel at Bath & Body Works
Facial cleanser	Kiehls	Dove face wash
Great allover body scent	Calvin Klein body wash	Victoria's Secret body washes
Reduced stretch marks	StriVectin-SD	Cocoa butter
Great body moisturizer	Crème de la Mer	Vaseline
Spa products	Bliss Spa products	True Blue at Bath & Body Works
Soft hands	Paraffin treatment	Vaseline and old cotton winter gloves
A great wax	Poetic Waxing Kit from Beauty.com	Sally Hansen Sugar Wax Hair Removal Kit
Cellulite reducer	Cellex-C	Avon skin-firming gel

purchased for $20 at the local DSW if you have crusty feet. It will be difficult for people to admire your Tiffany-inspired bracelet from Wal-Mart if your hands look like they should be sprouting a cactus. So copy down this list of fabulous beauty products to help you continue to look your best.

You can look like a million bucks without having to spend $110 on a one-ounce jar of Crème de la Mer by scheduling an appointment at a local beauty school. Budget fashionistas swear by the facials at the Aveda beauty schools. Not only do they use great Aveda products, but you can also get three months' worth of facials at the school for the price of one at an expensive spa; in addition, an instructor monitors all sessions. Find the Aveda salon nearest you by visiting Aveda.com.

Budget Fashionista Tip #18: How to Save Money on Haircuts

A great haircut can make or break a look. You could wear a potato sack and still look fabulous as long as your hair looks great. Is it possible to save money on haircuts? Yes! Look off the beaten path: Salons in ritzy areas often charge more to cover their expensive overheads. Pay attention to the products used and head to Ulta or Sally's Beauty Supply to obtain these products to prolong the cut. Also try the following:

- Find someone who is a great stylist but travels and doesn't have a chair in a salon. This stylist will be cheaper because he or she doesn't have to pay for chair rental and can come to your home or office for a cut.
- Visit salons in your price range and watch how they cut hair. Then choose the best stylist at the salon.
- Pay for a major stylist but go only two to four times per year. Have a cheaper stylist maintain the look.

Also ask if the stylist or salon has any special discount times or days. Many salons will give you a discount if you come on traditionally slow days such as Tuesdays or Wednesdays or if you are willing to come in midmorning.

My Favorite Beauty Product: Vaseline

African-American women swear by Vaseline. As a young African-American woman, my grandma Doonie handed the beauty secrets of Vaseline down to me. It must work, because you would be hard-pressed to find a single wrinkle on her eighty-two-year-old face. Go into any African-American home, and I guarantee you will find at least one (probably two) jars of Vaseline. I'll bet you Oprah has a few lying around, and Condoleezza Rice probably has one stashed in a White House bathroom. Vaseline is as much a part of the fabric of African-American life as sweet potato pie and *The Cosby Show*.

You don't have to be an African American to benefit from the magical beauty powers of Vaseline. I use Vaseline as a cheaper and better alternative to paraffin treatments by slathering large amounts on my hands and feet and then wrapping them in hot towels for five minutes. It's a wonderfully quick moisturizing treatment. I also use it on scrapes and cuts and as an emergency hair gel. Below are some other uses for Vaseline:

- To soften rough feet. Soak feet in a pan of warm water for fifteen minutes. Remove feet from water and exfoliate with a pumice stone. Slather on a generous amount of Vaseline, throw on a pair of your thickest white socks, and head to bed.
- To make smiling easier. Beauty pageant participants put a small amount between their upper lip and gums.
- As a last-minute shoe polish. Smear a small dab on the toe of the shoe and lightly spread it around the entire shoe. Don't use too much because it may damage the leather.
- As a lip gloss. Place a small amount in an old contact case and mix it with leftover lipstick to create your own.
- As a gel to groom and hold eyebrows in place.
- To style and hold hair in place instead of using a gel.
- To help soothe sunburn.
- To prevent windburn on cold, windy days.

Turn Your Kitchen into a Home Spa

My grandma may have taught me all about the budget beauty power of Vaseline, but it was my mom who taught me how to whip up amazing beauty products right from our fridge. The contents of your kitchen cabinets will have you looking like a million bucks at a fraction of the price of a day at the spa. Note: Don't try any of these home remedy treatments if you are allergic to any of the products, and always test mixtures on a small patch of skin at least forty-eight hours before to make sure you have no allergic reactions.

The beauty (pun intended) of turning your kitchen into a spa is that it is the perfect reason to invite friends over for a party. Have each friend bring a product from their fridge and spend the day making your own facial and hair masks. Eat whatever is left over.

Facials

Water plus eucalyptus to refresh skin: Add eucalyptus or tea tree oil to a pot or bowl of boiling water. Put a towel over your head and place your face over the steam.

Tomato paste to clean pores: Pour a can of tomato paste into a bowl and heat it in the microwave until lukewarm. Spread on your face and let set for five minutes, then wash off.

Scrubs

Honey plus oatmeal for dry skin: Mix ½ cup of plain uncooked oats with 3 tablespoons of honey. Apply to face, let set for fifteen minutes, and then rinse thoroughly. (Sometimes I like to warm the mixture a bit in the microwave, but if you do this, be careful that the oats don't start to cook.)

Cornmeal plus milk for acne: Add ½ cup of cornmeal to ¼ cup of milk. Mix together to make a paste and scrub on the skin. Let set for ten minutes and then rinse.

Moisturizing Facial Scrubs

Olive oil plus sugar exfoliating scrub: Mix 3 tablespoons of olive oil with ½ teaspoon of sugar. Scrub on your face and then rinse with warm water.

Olive oil plus avocado moisturizer: Mix ½ avocado with 2 tablespoons of olive oil. Apply to face and leave on for ten minutes. Rinse thoroughly.

Body

Scented oil (lavender, peppermint) plus Epsom salts body scrub:
Mix approximately ¼ cup of oil with 1 cup of Epsom salts. Gently
scrub onto body using circular motions. Save any remaining mix in
a clean old jelly or pickle jar with the top tightly closed.

Moisturizing milk bath: Pour 1 gallon of whole milk into a bathtub.
Fill with water and add 1 cup of lemon juice. Soak for fifteen min-
utes. The milk softens your skin, and the lemon cleans your pores.
Make sure you take a cold shower afterward.

Oatmeal body scrub: Mix 2 cups of raw oats with one egg and one
mashed apricot. Mix well, apply to your skin as a scrub, and let set
for 15 minutes. Rinse with cold water. This exfoliates and tightens
the skin.

Avocado body moisturizer: Blend two whole avocados with ¼ cup
of olive oil. Massage into your skin for a great full-body moisturizer.
Rinse with warm water.

Soothing tea bath: Add eight bags of peppermint or chamomile tea
to a steaming bath. Sit back and relax.

At-Home Hair Treatments

Coloring

Kool-Aid: If you can't afford Manic Panic hair coloring, then cherry
or strawberry Kool-Aid is a great way to color your hair temporarily.
The resulting look is more punk than Prada, but it can create a good
retro effect. Mix one package of Kool-Aid with 2 cups of water. Use
it to rinse your hair. Repeat for deeper color or add more water for
less color.

Cheap Hair Rinses

Blondes: Steep three chamomile tea bags in 2 cups of boiling water. Drain and let cool. Use as rinse after shampooing.

Brunettes and redheads: Pour 1 cup of cranberry juice on your hair, let it set for ten minutes, and then rinse. You can also use cider vinegar to bring out the highlights in brown hair.

Conditioners

Dry hair: Combine ¼ cup of mayonnaise (the real stuff, not Miracle Whip) with 3 tablespoons of olive oil and one egg. Apply to hair, cover with a plastic cap, and wrap with a warm towel. Let set for fifteen minutes and then rinse and shampoo as usual. This conditioner works wonders on my dry hair and is perfect for the winter.

Dull hair: Mix ½ cup of lemon juice with ½ cup of water. Use it to rinse your hair and let it sit for five minutes. Rinse with cold water. Makes hair shiny and gives it a great smell. Perfect for the summer.

Beauty Sites

Before heading out to a local grocery store or CVS, check out these wonderful online beauty sites.

Beauty Information

Beaublog (www.beaublog.com). Blog dedicated to reviews of beauty products.

The Beauty Report (www.thebeautyreport.com). Maria Brown, former MUA and current stay-at-home mom, researches the best beauty products and tips and gives amazing personalized advice.

Cosmetic Connection (www.cosmeticconnection.com). This is the top site for beauty information on the Web.

Beauty Products from Your Grocery Store

Avocados: a great moisturizer and another key ingredient in home spa treatments

Cooking oil spray: for drying nails in a hurry

Cranberries: add flavor and color to homemade lip gloss

Eggs: great source of protein for hair and skin and used in temporary face-lift treatments

Honey: works wonders on zits and a key ingredient of facials

Milk: primary ingredient in many spa treatments

Oatmeal: great exfoliant and key ingredient in home spa treatments

Olive oil: a great moisturizer for dry hair and skin, and the key ingredient in many homemade spa treatments mentioned in this chapter

Paper cupcake holders: perfect for mixing foundation and/or lipstick

Plastic grocery bags: for wrapping shoes as well as products that might leak when traveling

Tomato paste: to tighten pores

Vegetable brush: a great, cheap body brush

White plastic gloves: provide strong protection for hands while coloring hair

Zippered plastic bags: perfect as cheap makeup bags or to hold breakable lotion bottles while traveling

The Budget Fashionista Beauty Trends Newsletter (www.thebudgetfashionista.com). Features the ten best beauty products each month, all for under $20.

Makeup Alley (www.makeupalley.com). Great site for up-to-the-minute beauty advice, product reviews, and more.

Beauty Products

Aveda (www.aveda.com). Aveda products are a natural way to protect your skin and enhance your natural beauty. Plus, when you purchase something from the store, they give you a free mini hand massage.

Avon (www.avon.com). Has the best beauty products for the bucks. Skin-So-Soft continues to be a summer must-have, and the Mark line of beauty products rivals department store products.

Beauty.com (www.beauty.com). Stocks the top beauty products from Philosophy, Nars, and more. This online store almost always has coupons.

Bliss Spa (www.blissspa.com). It may be hard to get an appointment at the spa, but you can obtain their excellent bath products at local department stores or online at blissspa.com.

Dove (www.dove.com). Focuses on real beauty for real women. It is the cheapest cleanser out there, and senior fashionistas swear by it. Their interactive Web tools are beyond addictive.

Good to Be You (www.goodtobeyou.com). Carries a diverse range of hard-to-find beauty products that will soon become your favorites. Plus, you'll have a blast browsing the site.

Lush (www.lush.com). Has a wide range of great-smelling, cruelty-free products. The rock star soap from this international beauty phenomenon goes well with my shower renditions of "Stairway to Heaven."

Ulta (www.ulta.com). Discounts galore at this beauty store chain. Their impressive collection of hair and spa products makes this the perfect source for "spa night" goodies.

Chapter 9

Trends and the Designers Who Love Them

ow that we've gotten the basics out of the way, it's time to develop the fun side of your wardrobe. Never, ever spend a lot on a trend. In fact, trendy pieces should not take up more than 30 percent of your clothing budget. Trends change much too fast for those of us on a budget to adapt to. Even if your personal style tends to be more trendy, you still shouldn't spend more than 30 percent on the trendy items. (We'll talk about how to do this later in the chapter.)

You can mix and match trendy pieces with the Perfect Ten to create unique looks. Classic style icons like Audrey Hepburn and, more recently, Nicole Kidman rarely follow trends; instead, they opt to wear items that reflect and enhance their own personal style. Think of your Perfect Ten as the cake and your trendy pieces as the icing—adding the little extra "oomph" to your wardrobe.

In this chapter you'll learn some of the tools that fashion stylists like me use in forecasting and uncovering the next big trend. You'll learn to always stay ahead of the style curve and find out how to save tons of money by purchasing the cheaper designer bridge lines.

What's a Trend?

A trend is a current style or the general direction in which fashion is moving. Stone-washed jeans were a trend. Bohemian skirts were a trend. Poodle skirts were a trend. Not all trends are short-lived, however. Denim jeans and T-shirts were both trends that are now closet staples.

Designers both influence and are influenced by trends. According to trend forecaster David Wolfe, designers look at social, economic, and political factors to predict the beginning of a trend. For example, the emergence of the miniskirt in the mid- to late sixties was influenced greatly by the women's movement. Musicians, movie stars, and other celebrities influence trends, too—such as the lace half gloves trend started by Madonna in the eighties and the baggy pants look inspired by hip-hop stars. It has also been reported that skirt length changes with the state of the economy (relatively shorter in a bad economy, relatively longer in a good economy).

Sometimes a trend emerges when a group starts wearing an item in response to a particular need. For example, surfers in Australia needed to stay warm and dry after coming out of the water, leading to the development of Ugg boots. Sometimes a trend develops as a way for a particular group of people to distinguish themselves or show status, like the early hip-hop artists, who wore big gold chains. Other times they come about in response to a particular marketing need by a company; those Pepsi and Coca-Cola rugby shirts popular in the mid-eighties are an example. (People, including myself, paid up to $80 to essentially advertise a soft drink company.)

Soon others in the general population start to observe the trend. In the case of the Ugg boot, the surfer culture has always influenced California style, so others in California started to wear the boots. Then shows like *The* OC featured the boots, and West Coast–based celebrities such as Kate Hudson and Pamela Anderson were photographed wearing them, increasing awareness of the trend around the country. Wanting to emulate their favorite celebrities, lots of people went out and bought the boots, creating a frenzy for the shoe and making it difficult to obtain a pair.

Trends for Cheap

Don't go out and blow your entire check on a trend that will be out of style by the time your rent is due. Head to these stores for designer-influenced pieces at dirt-cheap prices:

Asos.com (www.asos.com). Britain-based site with very affordable "designer-inspired" clothing; organizes its collection by celebrity styles

Avon (www.avon.com). This beauty giant also sells current fashions.

Bluefly.com (www.bluefly.com). *the* place to score genuine designer pieces for up to 80 percent off retail prices

Charlotte Russe (www.charlotterusse.com). a well-designed store featuring "of the moment pieces" for well under $30

Forever 21 (www.forever21.com). trendy items for well below fashion editorial prices

H&M (www.hm.com). the ultimate destination for cheaper versions of the hottest runway looks

La Redoute.com (www.laredoute.com). French fashion sensibilities at Wal-Mart prices

Old Navy (www.oldnavy.com). trendy items in a wide range of sizes at prices you can afford

Rampage (www.rampagestores.com). fashion-forward items inspired by your favorite celebrities

Target (www.target.com). The Isaac Mizrahi and Mossimo lines are Budget Fashionista favorites.

Victoria's Secret (www.victoriassecret.com). fashion-forward jeans, tops, and more available online and via their catalog

Wet Seal (www.wetseal.com). stylish pieces and great accessories

Zara (www.zara.com). quality celeb-influenced clothing and good quality at reasonable prices

Trend vs. Staple

Getting the scoop on the latest fashion from your favorite magazine or from the front row of Fashion Week will help you find
trends, but to successfully build a functional wardrobe you must be
able to distinguish between a trend and a staple. A trend is a current style, and a staple is a timeless piece that is *always* in style, like
a pair of good-fitting jeans. Your Perfect Ten are excellent examples of staples. Use the guide below to help you distinguish between a trend and a staple.

Item	Trend	Staple	Why?
Boots	Shearling	Black leather knee-highs	The basic black leather boot has been a closet staple since the beginning of time. Its sleek, understated design makes it a classic.
Jeans	Low low-rise	Classic fit	Classic jeans fit more body types than the trendier low low-rise jeans.
T-shirts	T-shirts with written sayings	Regular style	Regular T-shirts can be worn by everyone, not just twelve-year-olds.
Earrings	Chandelier	Pearls	Chandelier earrings are fabulous, but pearls never go out of style. Pick a woman from any generation, and she will most likely have pearls in her jewelry box.
Shoes	4-inch (or more) stilettos	Standard 1½–2-inch heel	Stilettos are only as stable as the person wearing them.
Tops	Leather	White shirt	The white shirt looks as good with a pair of jeans as it does with a business suit.

Starting Your Own Trends

The problem with trends is that once they reach the mass market, you start to see them everywhere. One way to remain ahead of the fashion curve is to start your own trends, which will save you money as you purchase items before the demand (and price) increases. Develop your own trends based upon what you think will be the next "big thing." Here are some tips on how to find an emerging trend.

- **Turn to the streets.** Fashion designers often turn to the streets to find inspiration for their collections. Marc Jacobs hit big in the spring of 2001 with his Steven Sprouse graffiti-designed bags by Louis Vuitton. Juicy Couture sweat suits bear an eerie resemblance to the terry-cloth sweat suits worn by early hip-hop artists like LL Cool J. Watch music videos, particularly hip-hop music videos, to get a feel for how to be "ghetto fabulous." Head to your nearest urban center and observe what the young and hip are wearing, and don your own version of the trend.

- **Watch TV.** The popularity of hit shows like Fox's *The OC* and West Coast–based musicians like No Doubt foreshadowed the emergence of California style.

- **Put on your travel shoes.** When traveling, observe the local styles and pick up items that are indigenous to that place or culture. I've purchased some of my most fashion-forward pieces on trips to places like India, Toronto, and Wisconsin.

- **Observe social and economic cues.** Fashionable leather tote bags became popular when working women demanded a stylish alternative to the boring leather briefcase. With all of the recent attention placed on "metrosexuality," leatherwear and accessory companies like Jack Spade and Coach started to develop "murses," purses for men, to give men a stylish masculine bag to carry their PDAs, cell phones, wallets, and other items.

- **Do the exact opposite of what's "in."** Observe the current trends and do the exact opposite. If pointed-toed shoes are all the rage, then wear round-toed shoes. If miniskirts are in, wear floor-length skirts. At some point what you're wearing will come back in style, and you will be perceived as being trendy and fashion forward.

Starting your own trends is not for the faint of heart. You can be subject to much ridicule from your unenlightened fashion brethren, and the items may be hard to find. This approach to personal style is best achieved by budget fashionistas who are Trendy or are Urban Trekkers because their style dictates adherence to the latest trends. There is also the issue of falling in love with a trend you have successfully forecasted only to have the trend turn into a fashion faux pas.

The Worst Fashion Trends Ever:

Fake Louis Vuitton bags	Trust me, everyone knows it's a fake.
Stirrup pants	Unless you're on a foxhunt with Charles and Camilla, there is no reason to put these pants on your body.
Acid-wash jeans	Whoever invented these jeans must have been on acid.
Jelly shoes	Shoes that can double as lunch containers are a major fashion no-no.
Parachute pants	The remaining stock of these pants should have been burned after *Breakin' 2: Electric Boogaloo*.
Ugg boots	Expensive house shoes. Admittedly, I was a victim.
Bullet bras	"Look, Ma! My breasts are concealed weapons."
Jheri curls	The amount of activator sold in the 1980s could have moisturized the world's children.
Feather hair clips	*Dances with Wolves* meets *Flashdance*.

Biker shorts	I'm still looking for the one person who actually looked good in these shorts.
Eighties career suits	It's sad when Dustin Hoffman (remember the movie *Tootsie*?) looks better in a suit than you.
Low low-rise jeans	Some things are better left between you and your gynecologist.

Buh-bye: The End of a Trend

You can tell that a trend is over if you see "designer-inspired" versions of it at megastores like Wal-Mart. Mass-market retailers are interested in items that appeal to the masses and can sell in large quantities. If you see your grandma wearing a knockoff pair of a trendy shoe purchased from one of these retailers, most likely it isn't in style anymore.

The Budget Fashionista Explains: What to Do When Your Favorite Item Becomes a Fashion Faux Pas

I've been rocking brooches since Bill Gates was just a millionaire. I would search the local Salvation Army for great antique brooches and casually visit my grandmother to take a peek into her jewelry drawer. In elementary school I wore them pinned to the top button of my collar à la Molly Ringwald; in high school I wore them on my blazers; and in college I wore them in my hair like barrettes. When they came into fashion, I was ecstatic (great brooches everywhere) and hesitant (trends almost always become clichés). My worst fears were confirmed when in early 2005 my favorite accessory officially became a cliché.

So what's a budget fashionista to do when her favorite item becomes a cliché? Here are four options:

1. **Stop using or wearing it.** Stop wearing the item(s) for at least six months or as long as it takes for the antitrend backlash to pass.

2. **Wear it a different way.** Use the trend in a different manner than it was used before. For example, I took one of my winter pashmina scarves ($5 on the streets of New York City), wrapped it around my body like a makeshift poncho, and pinned it high on my shoulder with one of my brooches.
3. **Give it away.** Give it to some poor, unfashionable friend. You'll get it out of your closet and create goodwill.
4. **Wear it anyway.** Continue to wear the trend, daring anyone who gets in your path to challenge your fashion expertise.

Budget Fashionista Tip #19: Find a Celebrity Style Twin

If you don't have the patience to start your own trend, find a celebrity style twin. Celebrities pay big money for stylists, makeup artists, designers, and so forth, to help them look great and stay current. Find a celebrity whose style you admire and whose body type is similar to yours. Remember to practice Reality Dressing: If you wear a size 22, Halle Berry is not your style twin, but the fabulous comedienne MoNique would make a great style twin. Search for the star on the Web, in magazines, and in newspapers, and print out looks that you like. Put these styles in the look book you will create at the end of this chapter.

Use your celebrity style twin as a guide, but be careful not to go overboard in trying to emulate her fashion sense. Celebrities are the ultimate budget fashionistas—getting tons of free stuff even though they're the only ones who can really afford it. Almost all the stars you see walking the red carpet at big shows like the Oscars, Grammys, and Emmys get their dresses for free, and a select few get paid up to six figures to wear certain items. For example, Oscar-winning actress Hilary Swank was reportedly paid a high five-figure "fee" for wearing a piece of Chopard diamond jewelry to the 2005 Academy Awards.

Trendsetters: Designer Power

Coco Chanel, Karl Lagerfeld, Christian Dior, Calvin Klein, Marc Jacobs. What do all these folks have in common? They're all beloved designers who have made millions from their ability to instill desire in the hearts of fashionistas worldwide.

On the Site

It's helpful for a budget fashionista to have a general understanding of the top designers of the world. Visit TheBudgetFashionista.com and read my three-part Ultimate Guide to Designers. Review this list before you go to sample sales, thrift stores, and garage sales, and you'll be able to recognize a deal when you see it. For example, while doing my weekly shopping at a local Salvation Army, I found a pair of beautiful black pants by Marc Jacobs in wonderful condition for $4.99. If I had no idea who Marc Jacobs was, I would have missed out on an amazing deal.

Every budget fashionista must have at least one designer piece in her wardrobe—if for no other reason than bragging rights. Until recently there was no such thing as buying designer fashions while on a budget. In order to purchase a luxury item such as a Lanvin dress, you had to live in a major metropolitan area like New York or Los Angeles and be very wealthy. The rise of Internet shopping, outlet malls, and sample sales has made designer items available to the masses.

Expensive vs. Budget: Designer by Personal Style Type

Use the following chart to find designers and stores that fit your style and your budget.

Personal Style	Expensive ($100+)	Budget (less than $100)
Sporty	Ralph Lauren Collection, Anne Klein, Chaiken, Armani	Tommy Hilfiger, Jones New York, the Gap, J. Crew, American Eagle Outfitters
Trendy	Roberto Cavalli, Dolce & Gabbana, Versace, Dsquared, Heatherette	Forever 21, H&M, Express, Bebe, Torrid, Charlotte Russe, Rampage
Conservative	Oscar de la Renta, Dana Buchman, Ellen Tracy, Bill Blass	Talbots, Lord & Taylor brand, Ann Taylor, Liz Claiborne
Socialite	Chanel, Gucci, Lanvin, Givenchy, Dior	Banana Republic, Zara, The Limited, Club Monaco, Isaac Mizrahi for Target
Urban Trekker	Kenneth Cole, Donna Karan, Balenciaga, Marc Jacobs, Rock and Republic, Armani	DKNY, Dollhouse, Old Navy, A/X Exchange, Urban Outfitters
Romantic	Tracy Reese, Nanette Lepore, Kate Spade, Laura Ashley, Anthropologie	Ashley Stewart, Newport News, Daisy Fuentes line at Kohl's, Nine West clothing line

Thanks to the successful partnership of high-end designers like Issac Mizrahi with mass-market retailers like Target, budget fashionistas can find pieces from their favorite designers for significantly less than these designers' couture lines. Furthermore, these designers are now accessible to fashionistas who live outside of fashion centers. Head to your local JC Penney to find items from the Nicole collection by Nicole Miller. Stop by the local H&M to stock up on pieces by famed Chanel head Karl Lagerfeld or former

Chloe head (and Paul McCartney's daughter) Stella McCartney. Below is a list of top designers and their expensive and more budget-friendly lines.

Designers for Less (as of June 2005)			
Designer	**Expensive**	**Budget-friendly**	**Store**
Giorgio Armani	Giorgio Armani	A/X Exchange	A/X Exchange and department stores
Patricia Fields	House of Fields	Patricia Fields for Candies	Select department stores
Marc Jacobs	Marc Jacobs	Marc by Marc Jacobs	Barneys, Bloomingdale's
Nicole Miller	Nicole Miller	Nicole	JC Penney
Isaac Mizrahi	Isaac Mizrahi	Isaac Mizrahi for Target	Target
Donna Karan	Donna Karan black label	DKNY	Department stores nationwide
Cynthia Rowley	Cynthia Rowley	Swell	Target
Monet	Monet	Marvella	Target
Cacharel	Cacharel	Cacharel (for LaRedoute.com)	LaRedoute.com
John Paul Gaultier	John Paul Gaultier	John Paul Gauliter (for LaRedoute.com)	LaRedoute.com
Tommy Hilfiger	H by Tommy Hilfiger	Tommy Hilfiger	Department stores nationwide
Jennifer Lopez	Sweetface	J. Lo	Macy's and other department stores nationwide
Tracy Reese	Tracy Reese	Plenty by Tracy Reese	Department stores nationwide
Dolce & Gabbana	Dolce & Gabbana	D&G	Saks Fifth Avenue, Neiman Marcus, boutiques, and discount department stores
Tara Subkoff	Imitation of Christ	Tara Subkoff for Naturalizer	Naturalizer

Designer	Expensive	Budget-friendly	Store
Steve Madden	Steve	Steve Madden	Department stores and Steve Madden boutiques
Michael Kors	Michael Kors	MICHAEL by Michael Kors	Filene's, Lord & Taylor, and other department stores nationwide
BCBG Max Azria	BCBG Max Azria	Parallel	Sears
Anne Klein	Anne Klein	A Line	Sears
Ralph Lauren	Ralph Lauren Collection	Ralph Lauren (green label)	Department stores nationwide and discount department stores

The Budget Fashionista Explains: High vs. Low

It was a packed house at Isaac Mizrahi's June 2004 fashion show. Editors from the top magazines sat mesmerized as model after model paraded down the catwalk wearing high-priced items from his couture line paired with low-end items from his line at Target. After the show an editor from a major fashion magazine commented that the line was so blurred between the high-end and low-end items that she had a hard time discerning the differences between the two. Mizrahi effectively demonstrated to the die-hard "I only shop at Bergdorf" crowd what budget fashionistas have known all along: Mixing high end with low end is not only easier on the wallet but helps create a signature look.

When mixing higher-end items and lower-end items, don't worry about matching price points; focus on creating the outfit. I find it helpful to look at all my clothes as equal and then create outfits based on the look, not the designer. The plus of dressing high and low is that you create a unique style that looks effortless and costs a great deal less than dressing in designer from head to toe. Wear your Louis Vuitton Murikami bag with those Old Navy flip-flops. Mix the Prada dress with your Payless pumps. Don't be afraid to pair your Manolos with the skirt you bought at Kohl's last week.

Here's How to Pull Off the High-Low Look

Some stylists advocate using a certain formula like going high on pants and low on tops. This is a great formula if you happen to like pants. However, I tell my readers that your high-end pieces should always be your signature item. Spend money on the pieces that you like the most because you will wear them longer, getting more bang for your buck. Furthermore, your signature piece is the center of your personal style, your personal calling card. You should still look for your signature item on sale, but make sure it is of high quality and from a well-known designer.

The low-end items should be fillers like jeans (unless jeans are your signature piece). No one knows the difference between a great pair of Levi's and a pair of Seven jeans. It's the fit that matters. Spend little on T-shirts (Old Navy has the best T-shirts for the best price), trendy earrings (Claire's, Lord & Taylor, and Target all have great earrings at low prices), hosiery (you don't have to spend $20 on a pair of socks), sandals (DSW, Payless, and Nordstrom Rack all have a fabulous selection at reasonable prices), and items you rarely wear.

The Wonderful World of Knockoffs

Recently there's been quite a bit of debate regarding knockoff bags and the impact they've had on the fashion industry. I admit that I've purchased a knockoff or two in the past. Pretty much every fashionista has at one time or another. Knockoffs are the exact duplicate of someone else's products, and in some ways it isn't fair to the designers. Imagine spending years perfecting your art, only to have someone steal your idea and sell it for well below market value. On the other hand, fashion designers borrow elements of popular design all the time. For example, everyone has made Chanel-inspired jackets, from Prada to DKNY to Wal-Mart's George line. So what's the difference between these copies and the original Chanel jacket? Designer-inspired versions don't try to pass themselves off as Chanel.

Some designer bags are simply not worth the price. Never compromise quality for style. No matter how cool you might think the bag looks, no designer—not even Karl Lagerfeld—can make a fabulous bag out of inferior materials. It just can't be done. As a budget fashionista you don't have the luxury of recklessly purchasing high-priced items. Don't spend $500 on a nylon bag just because it is

Budget Fashionista Tip #20: How to Spot a Fake Bag

The most popular question on TheBudget Fashionista.com involves how to spot a fake designer bag. Later in this chapter I'll give some ways to spot the most commonly knocked-off bag, the Louis Vuitton Monogram canvas bag. With regard to other designer bags, there are three simple ways.

1. **You bought it from a street vendor.** If you bought your bag from a street vendor, it's real—real fake (unless it was stolen). Designers don't sell their purses on the street in your local Chinatown.

2. **It sounds too good to be true.** You can't purchase a real, brand-new Prada nylon bag for $20. If you aren't buying it from a reputable dealer and it is more than 50 percent off the retail price, proceed with caution. Make sure you can purchase the item using a credit card with buyer protection and that the site or store has a liberal return policy.

3. **The quality is poor.** Most high-end designer bags are expensive because of the high quality of workmanship (although a few are expensive just because of the name). If you're concerned about the quality of your bag, check to see if the seams are uneven, if the logo is blurry, if the leather is of poor quality, or if the serial number or date code is missing. If anything looks suspicious, take it to the designer's boutique or to a major department store like Saks Fifth Avenue or Neiman Marcus to see if they can help you determine whether or not it's real. However, there is a major downside: If your bag is found to be fake, the store may confiscate the purse, and you may be interviewed by the police concerning your purchase.

from a designer when you can spend $200 on a high-quality leather bag that will last you a lifetime.

There are times when you might want to buy a knockoff—and I'm not encouraging or discouraging you to do so—but if your goal is to buy a designer bag because you've always admired that designer's products, then by all means start adding extra dough to your shopping savings account until you have enough to purchase the real thing. If your goal is to impress others or emulate your favorite celebrity, however, you might want to explore the lower-cost alternative. The rule of thumb is never to pay more than $100 for a designer-inspired bag. With the advent of online outlets like Overstock and Bluefly, you can purchase the real deal for up to 80 percent off the retail price. Plus you will be able to wear it with pride, knowing that you have the real thing.

Legitimate Knockoffs

ABS by Allen Schwartz. ABS copies designer dresses worn by stars at the big award shows and sells them to stores like Macy's, Bloomingdale's, Smartbargains.com, and Bluefly.com for well below the price of a designer original.

Club Monaco. This store carries quality fashions inspired by the likes of Chanel, Prada, and Armani. My friend Malinda swears by their pants.

H&M. This store has been known to copy looks straight off the runways of Fashion Week. With special lines from Karl Lagerfeld, Stella McCartney, and other big designers, this store is a great place to score designer goods at mall prices.

Hype Bags. Well-made real leather bags inspired by designers like Marc Jacobs and Balenciaga.

XOXO. This clothing and accessories company reproduces designer-inspired versions of Dooney & Bourke and Marc Jacobs, usually made of pleather or some other man-made material.

The Budget Fashionista Explains:
Is My Louis Vuitton Bag Fake?

I can't tell you how many times I get asked this
question. Listen: If you bought a Louis Vuitton
bag for $40 from a stand on the street, it's fake. Pe-
riod. No discussion needed. Louis Vuitton doesn't
have authorized street resellers.

Carrying a fake Louis Vuitton makes you look like one big walk-
ing cliché. Most people assume that a Louis Vuitton Monogram
Canvas bag is fake even if it's real. So, why bother purchasing the
fake *or* the real thing? My advice: Head to the nearest Loehmann's,
Marshalls, Off 5th, Saks Fifth Avenue Outlet, or Last Call Neiman
Marcus and purchase a real high-quality bag (Coach, Longchamp,
Cole Haan, and Kenneth Cole all have great bags) and put the
money you save into your retirement account.

If you must purchase a Louis Vuitton Monogram bag, here are
some additional hints to determine whether or not your bag is fake:

1. If it claims to be brand-new and costs less than $300, most
    likely it is fake.
2. If the "LV" logo is upright on both sides, it might be a fake.
    (Check with a Louis Vuitton boutique regarding your specific
    bag.)
3. If it is brand-new and being sold on eBay or Yahoo! Auctions,
    there is a good chance it's fake.
4. If the piping is not leather, it is fake.
5. If the seams are uneven or frayed, or if the monogram is off or
    the bag is poorly sewn, it is definitely fake.
6. If there is no date code (also known as a date number) or if the
    seller is reluctant to provide a date code or receipt, it could be
    fake.
7. If it's a new bag and the color of the leather handle is different
    from that of the piping, it's fake.
8. If the seller doesn't allow returns, most likely it's fake.
9. If you bought it in your local Chinatown or from a street ven-
    dor, it's fake.

10. If the dustcover has rounded edges or the bag doesn't come with a dustcover, it's fake.
11. If the bag has a hanging tag (of any type) or a bright yellow tag or envelope, it's definitely a fake.

For more information on how to tell the authenticity of your Louis Vuitton bag, visit an authorized Louis Vuitton retailer or a boutique at your local high-end mall, call the Louis Vuitton headquarters at 212-758-8877, or visit My Poupette (www.mypoupette .com), a site dedicated to the promotion of real LV bags. Before buying your Louis Vuitton or other designer bag outside of an authorized retailer, do a little homework. Go to Saks Fifth Avenue, Neiman Marcus, or Bloomingdale's to look at the real thing. See how the bags are stitched together. Check to see if there's a registration, registration number, or date code. Examine how and where the label is placed in the bags. Observe how the straps are connected to the body. See what type of fabric or grain of leather is used. Be bold and ask the salesperson how to tell a fake from a real purse.

Budget Fashionista Tip #21: When to Buy the Real Thing

As a budget fashionista, you must know when to splurge and when to be frugal. Splurge on classic items like a good black suit in a flattering cut, a great A-line black dress, or a fantastic coat. Also splurge on items you've always wanted, such as a designer bag or a fur coat. If you're on a tight budget, don't splurge on a pair of Gucci leg warmers. Instead, focus on building a collection of timeless pieces.

Fashionable Flashback

I had wanted a Burberry trench coat ever since I first saw Kate Moss sashaying down the cobbled streets of London in a Vogue Burberry ad. They cost more than $1,000, so I never thought I would actually be able to afford one until I headed to Woodbury Commons Premium Outlet Center. It was late winter 2005, and for the past two months I *had been planning a trip to the legendary outlet mall, located about one hour outside New York City. Woodbury houses the outlets of some of the top designers in the world—Judith Leiber, Burberry, Prada, Etro, Bottega Veneta, and more. What began as a four-person adventure slowly dwindled to a solo expedition as my friends dropped out for various reasons. I have no problem shopping by myself, so I gassed up the Saturn and hit the highway for the designer outlet mecca.*

From the moment I entered the outlet complex, I was on a roll, buying a pair of Kenneth Cole pony hair black flats for $39.99, a pair of brown Mary Jane wedges from Via Spiga for $29.99, a DKNY jean jacket, and an Ellen Tracy white sailor jacket for under $20. I also bought two pairs of Kate Spade pumps for $60 apiece. As I left the Kate Spade outlet, the sign for the Burberry outlet caught my eye. On a whim I headed to the store.

At the Burberry outlet I was greeted immediately by a friendly, although frazzled, woman named Annie. Thinking that even at its outlet store the coats would be at least $800, I decided to humor myself and try on a coat. Annie went away and came back with the classic Burberry floor-length, double-breasted trench coat with removable wool lining and collar.

As I admired the perfect-fitting coat in the mirror, I thought about how many items I would have to sell on eBay to purchase it. I decided to check out the price tag: It was marked down from $1,085 to $450. Even though $450 is almost three times as much as I would normally spend on a coat, its classic style and cut made it a piece that I knew I would have for years. Plus, if I needed some quick cash, I could sell it to a consignment shop for close to what I paid for it. I pulled out my Visa debit card and headed to the checkout counter.

Finding Out What's Hot—the Cheap Way

You don't have to be in the front row at Fashion Week to find out what's in style. There are several cheap ways to find out what's in, such as visiting online style sites (for example, style.com and lucrie.com) as well as tuning in to television shows (Style Network's *The Look for Less*). The following is a list of great resources—for FREE fashion information.

The Best Free Sources for Fashion Information

The New York Times Fashion & Style section (www
.nytimes.com/pages/fashion). The legendary style
section of one of the world's most respected papers
will give you the scoop on what's hot before it hits your
street. Read Bill Cunningham's "On the Street" and be inspired by
the featured fashionistas.

Fashion.telegraph (www.telegraph.co.uk/fashion). Hilary Alexander
is one of my favorite fashion columnists. This Brit really knows her
stuff and gives a unique perspective on fashion from across the pond.

New York magazine (www.newyorkmetro.com/shopping). Get the
latest scoop on fashion from the online component of the hip *New
York* magazine. The Look Book section gives you a glimpse into the
personal style of everyday New Yorkers.

Style.com (www.style.com). *Vogue* and *W*'s online magazine offers
fashion editorials, style features, and streaming videos and pictures
from around the globe—all for free. They also have a series of articles on style icons like Cher, designer Elsa Schiaparelli, and Jackie
Onassis.

Daily Fashion Report (www.lookonline.com). This site gives you
the lowdown on the fashion industry, from trend reports to magazine launches to fashion commentary.

Fashion Week Daily (www.fashionweekdaily.com). Beyond snarky,
this is the insider's guide to the good, the bad, and the ugly of fashion.
The Daily is the best resource for fashion-related gossip and reviews of
Fashion Week. Run by the folks who publish *Fashion Week Daily*, the
official Fashion Week magazine, this site is a must-read for fashionistas
who can't make it to the tents of Fashion Week but still want to be in
the know. Make sure to sign up for their fabulous e-newsletter.

Factio Magazine (www.factio-magazine.com). If you're a fashion
junkie, then this site should be at the top of your bookmark list. It

features articles and pictures from major Fashion Weeks all around the world.

Local library. Your local library probably carries most of the top fashion magazines. Speak with your librarian to see if you can buy the outdated issues.

The Budget Fashionista (www.thebudgetfashionista.com). The site that launched this book. I dish fashion, beauty, and shopping tips along with a listing of the hottest sales and shopping events across the country. You will also find exclusive coupons for your favorite online stores.

Budget Fashionista Tip #22: Use Really Simple Syndication (RSS) Feeds to Get Your Free Fashion Info Daily

Really Simple Syndication (RSS) feeds post the headlines of your favorite blogs and news sites to your My Yahoo! or My MSN homepage or to an RSS reader, allowing you to manage all your free online fashion resources. To add a site to your MSN or Yahoo! homepage, follow these instructions: Log onto your My Yahoo! page and click on the "Add Content" tag at the upper left-hand corner of the page (right under the search bar). Search for the desired source, and when you find it, click "Add." You'll get the Yahoo! feed instantly on your My Yahoo! homepage. For My MSN, locate the "Add Content" box on the My MSN homepage, search for the desired source, and click "Add." To add a site to an RSS reader, follow the reader's instructions.

The following top fashion sites have RSS feeds:

The Budget Fashionista (www.thebudgetfashionista.com)
The New York Times Fashion & Style section (www.nytimes.com/pages/fashion)
Fashion Week Daily (www.fashionweekdaily.com)
fashion.telegraph (www.telegraph.co.uk/fashion)
The Washington Post Style section (www.washingtonpost.com)
Style.com (www.style.com)

Print Magazines as a Source of Trends

Whether it's in the grocery store checkout line or through a subscription, magazines are one of the best places to learn about new trends. If you feel the urge to splurge on a few magazine subscriptions, then it's best to stick with such staples as *Vogue*, *Bazaar*, and *W*. To save money, concentrate on buying the major fall issue (September) and the spring/summer issue (January/February). These issues usually feature most of the upcoming season's collections.

Start a Magazine Swap

To save money on magazines, start a magazine swap with a group of friends. Each person orders a subscription to a major fashion magazine, keeps the magazine for a week, and then swaps it for another magazine. That way you still get to review all the latest styles at a fraction of the price. The best place to buy them is online at sites like Magazine.com where you can get them for up to 90 percent off the retail price.

Potential Choices for Your Magazine Swap

Elle. Beautiful fashion spreads that focus on style for the trendier gal. This is the perfect place for up-to-the-minute information on beauty and fashion trends.

Harper's Bazaar. This classic high-end fashion magazine targets women of all ages and offers some of the best fashion editorials in the business. Although budget is considered $150 for a top, it is an excellent place to learn about classic styles. The magazine often profiles top fashionistas like Lee Radziwill (Jackie O.'s sister) and actress Chloe Sevigny. Interestingly, *Bazaar* has one of the lowest yearly subscription rates of any fashion magazine.

Lucky. The leader of the shopping magazine pack, *Lucky* doesn't necessarily show you what to wear but acts more as a catalog of the latest styles and products. Occasionally a good budget pick can be found, and it's a great guide for planning your shopping trips.

Marie Claire. This is like the little sister to *Vogue* and *Bazaar*. It features great editorials on how to duplicate popular looks for less. The magazine also features stories on important issues affecting women around the world, helping fashionistas be both stylish and socially conscious at the same time.

Shop Etc. While *Lucky* focuses more on products than stores, *Shop Etc.* tends to focus more on stores than products. It has the best spreads of any of the shopping magazines.

Vogue. The bible of fashion where the ads are sometimes better than the fashion editorial. Nothing is affordable, but its breathtaking spreads by the top designers continue to influence generations of fashionistas. The real reason to read the magazine, however, is for editor at large André Leon Talley's editorial notes, which make you feel like a socialite. Exceptionally fashionable, A.L.T. is the only six-foot-four-inch man in the entire world who could wear a pair of loafers with a velour tracksuit and look chic. He was schooled in the art of fashion by Diana Vreeland herself and introduced Melania Trump to Paris couture. A.L.T. is also the personal style tutor to celebrities, such as rapper Andre 3000 of OutKast, and is the only "fat" person liked by *Vogue* editor in chief Anna Wintour.

W. This magazine put the *haute* in haute couture. The 11-by-14-inch format is much like a fashion stylist's portfolio with beautiful fashion editorials featuring some of the world's most popular designers.

Women's Wear Daily. This is what the folks in the fashion industry read. It gives the complete inside scoop on the business end of the industry. A subscription is pricey ($150 plus for print, $99 for online), so I advise signing up for their free newsletter that contains the top industry headlines. It can be found on their site (www.wwd.com).

Some Other Great Magazines

Budget Living: tips and inspiring spreads on living fabulously for less
Essence: how the sistas do it
GQ: the classic men's style magazine

Jane: witty columns and fun spreads that appeal to the under-twenty-five set

The New York Times Magazine (insert in the Sunday newspaper): fashion, New York style

Paper: cutting-edge fashion and commentary for the "in" crowd

Ready Made: what do-it-yourselfers read

V Magazine: the more accessible version of the quarterly magazine *Visionaire*

Budget Fashionista Tip #23: Developing a Look Book

Remember all those items you circled in your favorite magazines for the exercise earlier in this book? You're going to use those pictures to develop a look book. Look books are binders or portfolios used by modeling agencies, designers, and merchants to display pictures of their new lines, top models, and bestselling merchandise. As a budget fashionista you're going to create a look book to help you translate the *Vogue* styles you love to a Target budget. Cut out pictures of styles that you love and paste them in a ring binder, folder, or regular lined notebook. Make sure you note any specific things that you like, including colors and/or fabrics. Take this book with you when you go shopping to help you find the higher-end styles shown in magazines in your favorite budget shopping haunt. This is particularly helpful for those who don't have much time to shop or who don't like to shop, because it gives sales associates a clear picture of your style needs. It's also helpful in assisting tailors and seamstresses in re-creating designer looks.

Fashionable Friends: Ultimate Source of Free Fashion Information

Highly fashionable friends are a great source of free fashion information because they act as style consultants, giving you solid advice and fashion direction based on their knowledge of your personal style. In addition, these friends are often "in the know" and have the latest scoop on the next big sale or major shopping event in your city. Below is a list of some potential fashionable friends:

Employees at your favorite stores. There is no bond stronger than the bond between a budget fashionista and the employees at her favorite store. Cultivating and maintaining relationships with these friends is critical in saving you major dollars. These angels understand your style, and you understand their commission structure. They call you weeks before a big sale and scour the celebrated stockroom—the place where they process items before placing them on the sales floor—to find you fashion goodies before they are placed on the floor. Since you're a "friend," they let you use their "friends and family discount" for an extra percentage off.

Rich, fashion-obsessed fashionistas. These fashionistas wouldn't be caught dead in the same thing twice and have a Hermès Birkin bag for every day of the week. They feel compelled to give their less financially fortunate friends their barely used castoffs, which you gladly accept. They also invite you to parties that have great swag (free gifts).

Fashionable Flashback: My Fashionable Friend Lloyd

I was a lowly high school sophomore when Mr. Lloyd, an incredibly fashion-forward junior, walked into my life. Actually, he didn't so much walk as glide across the floor, sort of like a black, gay Midwestern Norma Desmond. While everyone else at our high school looked like something the Gap threw up, Lloyd channeled the spirits of his sexually oppressed forefathers and foremothers and created a personal style that was the complete antithesis of our Midwestern roots. He wore black from head to toe—jeans, scarves tied around his head, even eyeliner. He was New York, while the rest of the students at Washburn Senior High were plainfully Minnesota.

Lloyd and I became friends because of our love of fashion and our disgust with the social and fashion limits imposed by our Midwestern high school. It was Lloyd who taught me how to apply eyeliner (during a particularly boring lecture on diction in twelfth-grade speech class) and encouraged me to develop my own personal style, "ghetto preppy." He had a strange but highly entertaining obsession with Diana Ross. During physics he would make me promise that when I became a big star he would be the Bob Mackie to my Diana Ross. He then proceeded to design for me an entire evening gown collection on the back of our physics homework.

When I moved from Minnesota to New Jersey, Lloyd was my only high school friend who dared to come visit me at my frat-boy-infested college wearing a black bob wig (which he slept in) and a fire-red blazer (which was fierce). He took me to my first concert at Radio City Music Hall (to see Diana Ross, of course), where we sat ten rows from the stage and a couple of seats away from the very fabulous RuPaul.

To this day Lloyd remains one of my most stylish friends. We eagerly trek through Chelsea during New York City blizzards in an effort to find such items as a vintage black dress for less than $20, and swap tips on men. He appreciates my fixation with flower bags and understands the importance of a great haircut. He loves shopping more than I do and doesn't hesitate to tell me when an outfit makes me look "negative," making him an invaluable friend.

The Fashion Olympics: Fashion Week

Fashion Week is when designers from Jennifer Lopez to Christian Dior to Oscar de la Renta show off their new designs for the upcoming season. There are several Fashion Weeks throughout the world, but the top shows are Milan and Paris (mostly couture), Tokyo and London (edgier fashions), New York (more ready-to-wear), and Los Angeles (more casual, laid-back). Also, several other cities—Atlanta, Johannesburg (South Africa), Miami, Chicago, and San Francisco—have their own versions of Fashion Week.

In the United States, New York City's Fashion Week is arguably the most anticipated fashion event of the year. It is held twice a year in really big white tents ("the tents") at Bryant Park (Forty-second Street between Fifth Avenue and Avenue of the Americas in Manhattan). Not all designers hold their shows at the tents. Some big designers who have a huge following, and designers who can't afford the sometimes $100,000-plus price tag of having a show at the tents, prefer to hold their shows in other locations.

During Fashion Week, fashion is secondary to the schmoozing. The shows last about fifteen minutes, so there has to be another reason that people flock to the tents. It is about seeing people and being seen. It is about having a seat versus standing in the crowded aisles. It is about who is in the front row versus who didn't score an invite. It is about collecting goodie bags and figuring out where to store the free *Women's Wear Daily* they shoved in your face.

The Budget Fashionista Explains: The Goodie Bag

A goodie bag is filled with swag—that is, free products, samples, postcards, and other items given to the attendees of events. You can score these bags at major charity events, restaurant openings, exclusive parties, and Fashion Week shows. Not all events have them, but all events that matter do.

The quality of the contents of the goodie bag is a direct result of who is sponsoring the party. If a major corporation is sponsoring the event, expect pins, T-shirts, and even travel pillows with the company's logo. If a major beauty company is sponsoring it, expect samples (and sometimes full-size items) of whatever product it's trying to promote. Scoring a goodie bag can be tricky at events that segment them according to importance. In some Fashion Week shows, for example, only those in the front row get goodie bags while the rest of us can barely get the show's program. If you're invited to a show or event that segments their goodie bags and you aren't deemed "important" enough to receive one, wait until the end and then scoop up the leftovers.

Fashion Weeks are usually held several months before the actual season they are showcasing to give buyers and magazines the chance to view the collections with enough lead time to stock their stores and write their articles, respectively. Invitations to these shows are usually limited to high-powered and high-moneyed fashionistas, celebrities, fashion writers and photographers, those who write about or photograph high-powered and high-moneyed fashionistas, and those with connections. Fortunately for me, I am a "Z-list" celebrity, falling somewhere between Alice from *The Brady Bunch* and your high school prom queen. I get invited to some shows, but not all of them.

There are several ways those of us without trust funds or celebrity status can score invitations to Fashion Week.

1. **Get credentialed.** If you have a website, blog, or a really good book report, you can apply for press credentials ($55 at www .olympusfashionweek.com). Applying for press credentials does not guarantee that you will actually get credentialed, however, and being credentialed does not guarantee you a seat at one of the top shows unless you work for *Elle, Vogue,* or some other top magazine. It merely puts you and your credentials on a list distributed to fashion show organizers.

2. **Volunteer.** I've never been a volunteer, but I imagine that it entails lots of running errands, fetching water, working crowd control, and possibly some janitorial duties. In exchange for your hard work you get to watch the shows, sometimes even meet the designers, and get a free T-shirt. Learn more at OlympusFashionWeek.com.

3. **Try to walk right in.** Getting into the lobby of the tents can be hard, but if you appear to be cool and "belong," you might be able to make it in. Once in, beg one of the PR folks at the registration table to let you watch the show (possibly standing). Before I was credentialed, I used to do this all the time, and I was able to watch the shows of Carolina Herrera, Calvin Klein, and Anna Sui. You will have better luck with the morning shows and shows of newer designers because, frankly, they need bodies to fill the seats. Before attempting this, study the calendar at Olympus Fashion Week and find out who the publicist is for the show. Don't expect this to work for a popular show like Heatherette or Oscar de la Renta, though.

I can't stress enough the importance of acting as if you belong and knowing at least the basics about the designer before trying to get into a show without an invite. Here is an example of what not to do. During the fall 2005 Fashion Week, I was rushing in for the Tracy Reese show when a father and daughter were making their way into the tents. By the way he was dressed, he could have been "of money," and his daughter was absolutely adorable. He was a total geek, however, when it came to trying to get into the show. He first asked the PR staffer what was going on (a sure sign that he didn't belong) and then, overlooking the big sign that read TRACY REESE, he asked what show was next. Needless to say, he and his daughter were booted out of the tents.

4. **Call the show's publicist.** According to an unethical but brilliant friend of mine, you could also try inventing a fake personal assistant and calling the show's publicist. Complain that your "boss" doesn't have a ticket and start to become very irate because obviously there was some oversight. Start to name-drop (Oprah, Simon Doonan), but make sure it's a relationship they can't trace. Don't say you are Oprah's best friend, because they will contact Oprah's publicist and you will be forever blacklisted from Fashion Week. You could say you're a producer of a hot new television show that hasn't premiered yet.

If you still can't get in, walk by the tents every day and pick up a free *Daily Report*—Fashion Week's daily magazine that gives you a wrap-up of the previous day's events and shows, as well as some pretty hilarious commentary. The magazines are free. Also spotted giving out free Fashion Week special issues is *Time* magazine and *Women's Wear Daily*. You might also be able to score free samples and other items from top designers.

Chapter 10

The Shopping List

You've uncovered your personal style. You've found your signature item. You know more about fashion than the editors of *Vogue*. You're now your own personal stylist.

To prepare you for the next and final step, knowing your bargains, you're going to take all the information you've gathered in this step and use it to develop a shopping list. It can be difficult for a budget fashionista to stay focused while shopping. Creating a shopping list is much like creating a grocery list: It helps you purchase only the items you need to fill your closet and fit into your budget. I suggest that you dog-ear this page (unless, of course, this is a borrowed book) because you'll refer to it quite often while reading about Step 3.

Here is an example of one of my shopping lists:

Kathryn's Spring Shopping List

Date:	*February 12, 2006*
My Shopping Budget:	*$300 per month*
Personal Style(s):	*Socialite and Trendy*
Body Shape:	*Hourglass*
Signature Piece:	*Great costume jewelry*

Favorite Pieces: *Burberry trench coat, turquoise beaded neck-lace, Old Navy Perfect Fit T-shirts, Nine West black trousers, Kenneth Cole flats*

True Shopping Confessions:
Personal Shopping Philosophies

As we get ready to head into "Step 3: Know Your Bargains," it's helpful to have a personal shopping philosophy, sort of like a guiding principle that helps direct your shopping activities. Mine is "Buy what you love and love what you buy." I asked the readers of TheBudgetFashionista .com to share with me some of their shopping philosophies:

"There is no point in paying retail when there's also T.J. Maxx."

"Spend more on good designer shoes and handbags. You can wear/carry them more than once a week without getting funny looks! Spend more on basics like black pencil skirts and white shirts. Get only a few new 'expensive' pieces each season and don't load up on trendy things."

"If you like it . . . buy it . . . ; otherwise you'll be thinking about it until you get it."

"Only one in ten purchases should be 'fad' items."

"Try to spend the most on items like handbags that aren't going to go out of style the next season . . . and also don't wear the same designer from head to toe."

"Make a list of what you need and first try to get those items."

"Value + Quality = Purchase."

"Rocker/Walker: If the item doesn't rock your world, then just walk."

My Shopping List

1. One pair of classic black pumps in a size 11 or European size 42
2. One pair of great-fitting jeans
3. Two cotton spandex shirts in any color except black or white
4. A white cotton collared shirt to replace my dingy old one
5. A new designer tote bag

Use all the information you've gathered about your personal style, fashion, etc., to develop your shopping list. Cut out pictures of the items on your list from major fashion magazines and place them in your look book. Head online to TheBudgetFashionista.com for tips and advice on developing your shopping list.

Your Shopping List

Date: _____

My Shopping Budget: _____

Signature Piece: _____

Personal Style(s):   *Sporty*   *Trendy*   *Conservative*
                      Socialite   *Urban Trekker*   *Romantic*

What I Need

1. _____

2. _____

3. _____

4. _____

5. _____

6. _____

7. _____

8. _____

9. _____

10. _____

Now, let's shop!

Step 3

Know Your Bargains

Telling a fashionista not to shop is like telling the sun not to rise. It's just not going to happen. Although fashionistas know how to shop, many don't know how to shop within a limited budget. There is a wonderful world of retail options available to help you realize your personal style without your having to arrange for a loan. And you don't have to live in New York City to find them.

In this step you'll take everything you've learned about budgets and bodies and go out into the world of shopping. I'll help you analyze every major type of store—from department stores to your local Goodwill—and give you the inside scoop on how and where to find the deals. You'll learn insider shopping tips from personal shoppers, and even hints on how to make your own necklaces.

By now you should feel pretty confident as an active consumer. You have your Visa gift card tucked nicely in your look book, which is overflowing with pictures of the styles you like. You have your shopping list and your most fashionable friend along for moral support and much-needed advice. Now all you need is a strategy.

Creating a Bargain Shopping Strategy

Every budget fashionista needs a shopping strategy. Think of yourself as the General Patton of budget shopping, storming the shores of retail stores to find the best deals. Before you attack your local bargain battlefield, you need to figure out your own shopping strategy, which works in connection with your shopping list. Your shopping list tells you what you need to buy, and your shopping strategy tells you how to buy it.

Shopping Strategy	Who It Works For	Why It Works	Where to Find Bargains
More quantity and less quality	Those who have nontraditional jobs (retail, part-time student positions, public relations, etc.) where being up to the moment and trendy is important	Fashion trends are constantly changing, and this strategy allows you to stay fashionable while on a budget.	Shop online at stores like Asos.com, fred-flare.com, Bluefly.com, and Coco-Delilah.com, and DIY sites like Lekkner.com. Also shop at popular mall-based stores like Forever21, Wet Seal, etc. Shop at sample sales and major sales at such stores as Barneys, Lisa Kline, Intermix, and Kirna Zabete.
Equal quality and quantity	Those who work in occupations where comfort and style are important like teachers, government and nonprofit employees, stay-at-home moms	Creates a balanced closet between trendy pieces (e.g., low low-rise jeans) and more conservative classic pieces (e.g., khakis).	Major mass-market stores like Marshalls, T.J. Maxx, and Filene's Basement. Big sale events and the clearance racks at local department stores, and online sites such as Nordstrom.com, Bloomingdales.com, etc.
More quality, less quantity	Those who work in traditional businesses such as banking, law, insurance, and other corporate environments where the standard dress is conservative and the perception of "success" is important	The French have this strategy down pat. By purchasing one or two quality pieces each year, you will develop a solid wardrobe of classic pieces.	The outlets of major designers (Furla, Chanel) and the outlets of high-end department stores (Neiman Marcus, Barneys, and Saks Fifth Avenue). Online at shops such as eluxury.com and yoox.com

Your shopping strategy is also closely tied to your personal style and occupation. If you work in a sales position, where image and status are key to the success of your job, then you will need to focus more on quality brand-name products than would a fashion assistant editor at a women's magazine who receives little pay and must stay ahead of the fashion curve. A teacher or stay-at-home mom who interacts with small children for most of her day shouldn't pay a great deal of money for designer threads that might get destroyed.

The Budget Fashionista Explains: The Definition of a Bargain

As a budget fashionista you must be able to differentiate between something that is a "bargain buy" and something that is just plain "cheap crap." The definition of a bargain differs depending on whom you ask, but in general it is finding a high-quality item that you would consider purchasing at its full retail price (or close to full price) for a much lower price. A bargain differs from an item that is cheap because in the case of the latter, the lower price is more a factor of poor quality than your shopping luck. For example, a fake Louis Vuitton bag is cheap; finding a real Louis Vuitton at a consignment shop for $100 is a bargain. Scoring a fully-lined black gabardine Theory suit for $50 is a bargain; purchasing an unlined black suit made of poor-quality rayon for $30 is cheap.

Quality is an important factor in assessing whether or not something is a bargain. Focus more on the value of the garment—a combination of price and quality—rather than on the brand name. Here is what you should look for to determine the quality of an item.

1. **See if the item is lined.** A lined garment is usually an indication that care has been taken in the making of the item, and it usually increases the cost of the garment. It also helps to prolong the wear of the garment by reducing friction between your body and the fabric, and it helps the garment maintain its shape.
2. **Check to see how the garment was dyed.** A sure sign that cotton has been cheaply dyed is to check the seams to see if you

can see the grieg (the grayish natural state of cotton). It's more expensive to dye the fabric of a garment than the garment itself after it has been constructed. If you see the grieg, the garment was constructed out of the raw, natural cotton fabric and then dyed.

3. **Feel the fabric.** How does the garment feel in your hands? Is it rough to the touch? Does it feel abrasive on your skin? If you answer yes to these questions, don't purchase the item. Some high-quality fabrics to look for are cashmere, tweed (make sure it's woven tweed), herringbone, and fine silk.

4. **Check the hem and seams.** All seams should be straight and strong when you gently pull the garment. Make sure the hem is even, that there is no puckering, and that there are no lumps in the hem. Give the seam of the garment a good pull to see if the seam unravels or comes a little loose. Also check to see if the hem was stitched or glued. Glued hems will come undone after repeated washings.

5. **Look at the shoulders.** Make sure the stripes and patterns on striped and patterned garments match throughout. A sure sign of cheap construction is when the print of the garment doesn't flow seamlessly.

Many of us are tricked into purchasing inferior items because of methods used by retailers. For example, they will add 99 cents to the cost of the item, making the item appear to be a dollar less than it actually is. It has also been proven that the selective use of SALE signs influences us to purchase items regardless of whether they are actually on sale.* One of my favorite department stores is guilty of this practice. According to a salesperson at this well-known store, items arrive there automatically marked up and are instantly marked down 30 percent when they hit the sales floor to give the illusion that the items are on sale. If an item becomes popular, the store raises it to its original price.

As a budget fashionista, I love a good sale. The keyword is *sale*. In my book a truly good sale begins at 30 percent off. Anything less,

---

* Eric Anderson and Duncan Simester, "Mind Your Pricing Cues," *Harvard Business Review* 81(9), September 2003, 96–103.

don't waste my time. It's not the sale sign that drives me to purchase, it's finding the *sale*. It is going to the Prada sample sale and finding a Miu Miu tote for $45. It is finding a vintage Gucci baguette circa 1985 at the local Goodwill for $10. It's finding white oxford shirts at Macy's for $4.99. Behind every sale there must be a *find*. Nothing is more disappointing than walking into a store with a huge sale sign in the window and finding nothing but a smattering of tops and bottoms in size 0.

Here are a few ways to circumvent some of the retail tricks:

- When you see a price ending in 99 cents, automatically round it up to the next number.
- Look for signs that say CLEARANCE before signs that say SALE.
- Head straight to the hidden corners, which is where most stores place their most discounted items. Fellow fashionistas often hide deals from other shoppers in these corners.
- Never open a store credit card account based on a discount. Store credit cards often carry much higher interest rates than regular credit cards, and the discount is often less than the cost of the finance charges and the impact on your credit rating.
- Before purchasing any item, ask yourself, "Why am I buying this shirt (pair of pants, shoes, etc.)?" If you can't think of an answer immediately, put the item back on the shelf.

Many stores, including some top discount department store chains and outlet stores, purchase special items—usually of significantly lower quality—to stock the stores. These items would never have been sold at the main stores. Remember to base your purchases on quality rather than name.

Chapter 11

Secrets of The Budget Fashionista

The Budget Fashionista's Top Shopping Secrets

Friends and readers of my website, TheBudgetFashionista.com, are used to my seemingly impossible fashion finds, like the Jean Paul Gaultier shirt I found for 99 cents at my local Salvation Army and my purchase of a pair of cream-colored Kate Spade sandals for $13.98. However, it was purchasing eleven pairs of shoes from DSW for $120 that cemented my place in the Budget Shoppers Hall of Fame.

The Budget Fashionista's Top Ten Greatest Fashion Finds (So Far)

1. Ugg boots, $25, on eBay.com
2. Max Mara knit top, $24.99, at Daffy's
3. Kate Spade sandals, $13.98, at DSW
4. Two Norma Kamali dresses, $2.49 apiece, at the Salvation Army
5. Tom and Linda Platt evening dress, $75 (retail price: $1,500), Off 5th, Saks Fifth Avenue Outlet
6. Jean Paul Gaultier knit top, 99 cents, at the Salvation Army
7. Brown Via Spiga Mary Janes (in size 11), $29.99, at Via Spiga outlet

8. Classic leather Coach tote bag, $50, at Coach outlet store
9. Three-quarter-length fox fur coat, $30, at Goodwill
10. Brand-new Gap jeans, $3.99, at the Gap

You don't have to be a bargain savant to find great deals. As The Budget Fashionista, I've learned quite a few tricks by keeping an ear to the dressing room door and my eyes on the runway, thus learning about new designers and new trends before they happen. I send birthday and holiday cards to all my fashionable friends so they'll keep me posted on exclusive shopping events like the Chanel sample sale. Then I use my top-secret shopping skills to find the items for well below retail price. Here are a few of my secrets.

Budget Fashionista Secret #1: Bargain for EVERYTHING

Budget fashionistas bargain for *everything*. Commit this rule to memory: There is no such thing as a set price, even at major department and chain stores. Always ask for a discount or special deal; the worst that can happen is that they say no, and then you're right back at square one. You can even negotiate a discount at thrift stores like the Salvation Army. Many stores give their managers the option of giving additional discounts on damaged items (usually up to 20 percent off), but some stores also give some leeway regarding undamaged regularly priced items as well. I encourage you to negotiate an extra percentage off for lipstick and pen marks on an item (just use the stain removal guide located in Appendix B to remove the stains). Your ability to get these additional discounts depends on a host of factors, the most important being your relationship with the manager and store employees.

In some shopping situations the sellers expect you to bargain—like at flea markets and garage sales. Few people are born with bargaining skill, and it does take some time to develop. The key is to find the bargaining process that works best for you. Below is an example of a process I use to bargain at these types of shopping venues:

1. **Identification.** I casually walk past the item, showing a little interest—just enough to indicate to the merchant that I'm considering the item. It's key at this stage not to show any enthusiasm. Be very nonchalant even if it's a Balenciaga bag for $40. I usu-

ally channel the spirit of Martha Stewart: calm, cool, and col-
lected. While I'm getting in touch with my inner ice queen, I
calculate the highest price I'm willing to pay for the item.

2. **Inquisition.** After I determine the highest price I'm willing to
pay, I ask the salesperson the cost of the item. I *never* indicate
how much I'm willing to spend. In negotiations the first person
who mentions a number is usually the one who loses. Continue
channeling your inner ice queen. Any cracks in your bargaining glacier, and you can kiss your bargain good-bye.

3. **Give and go.** This is the final step of the process. After the
salesperson gives me a price, I *always* pretend that the price is
too high—even if it is much lower than my highest price. I put
the item back on the shelf, followed by a well-placed "Oh" or
"Hmmm" or "Oh, well," and I start to leave the stall or store.
Always leave the store on good terms and thank the salesperson.
Ninety percent of the time the salesperson will come shouting
after you with a much lower price than was first mentioned.
Then you've won.

Budget Fashionista Secret #2: Shop in the Children's Section

Shop in the children's section of your favorite stores, especially the
boys' department, for basic T-shirts, fitted blazers, preppy polos, and
jean jackets well below the price of similar items across the aisle in
the misses' section. This is a particularly good option for petite fashionistas or budget fashionistas who wear a size 12 and below.

Misses' and Boys' Sizes Conversion Chart (Sizes are approximate.)	
Misses'/Juniors' Size	Boys' Size
1/2	10
3/4	12
5/6	14
7/8	16
9/10	18
11/12	20

Budget Fashionista Secret #3: Shop High End, Buy Low End

I go to the more expensive stores to preshop for the latest styles and then hit the less expensive stores to buy similar styles for less. When trying on a garment at a higher-end store, notice the fit and the way it drapes. Notice any special stitching (overlock or simple straight stitch), whether the garment is lined, and whether there are cuffs. Rub the fabric between your fingers and notice if it is rough to the touch. Is it flexible? How does it feel against your skin? Read the instruction label to see what fabric was used to make it and how to care for it. Then head to less expensive stores to purchase the item, using the knowledge learned from preshopping at the more expensive stores.

Budget Fashionista Secret #4: Calculate the Cost per Wear

Not all bargains are created equal. Some are really spending traps in disguise. Calculating the cost per wear of an item before purchasing the piece will easily uncover the true value of an item. The cost-per-wear formula is: Total cost of the item ÷ estimated number of days you'll wear it = the cost per wear.

When I bought the Burberry trench coat for around $450, I knew that I would wear the coat about five months a year or about 100 to 150 days per year—during the spring months of March to May and during the early fall from September to October. I would wear it for at least five years, or a total of 500 to 750 days. That comes to a total cost per wear of 60 cents to 90 cents. The longer I wear the coat, the lower the cost per wear. On the other hand, I recently purchased a trendy scoop-necked Isaac Mizrahi top for $26 at a local Target. I will be able to wear it a total of only twelve times (twice per month for six months) before it goes out of style— a cost per wear of $2.17. Using the cost-per-wear formula, the Isaac Mizrahi top is more than twice as expensive as the Burberry coat.

Budget Fashionista Secret #5: Get Friends and Family Coupons

Developing friendships with the sales staff of your favorite store can also help you score coupons. Employees at most major department stores—Macy's, Bloomingdale's, Marshall Field's—and smaller stores like Ann Taylor and the Gap allow their favorite customers to use their friends and family discount. These coupons are available at least twice a year and usually offer discounts of 20 percent or more. According to image consultant Carol Davidson, the friends and family coupons are often better than the coupons offered in Sunday circulars because there are fewer restrictions on them. Here is a selected list of stores with friends and family coupons:

Ann Taylor	J. Crew
Armani A/X	Kenneth Cole
Banana Republic	Liz Claiborne
Bloomingdale's	Lord & Taylor
Champ Sports	Macy's
Clinique	Marshall Field's
Dana Buchman	Mexx
Dillard's	Neiman Marcus
Ellen Tracy	Nordstrom
Foley's	Proffitt's
FootAction	Red Envelope.com
Foot Locker	Reebok
The Gap	Saks Fifth Avenue

Budget Fashionista Secret #6: Try EVERYTHING On

I try on every piece of clothing I purchase—even if it's a $3 tank top at Wal-Mart. Time is money, and I would rather spend my time dishing great shopping tips than waiting in line to return something that didn't fit. My dedication to trying on every item has saved me hundreds of dollars in unflattering purchases, not to mention the money for gas that I would have spent returning the items to the stores.

This is especially important for busy people with little time to shop. Think about how difficult it is for you to take time out of your day to shop and think of the difficulties you have finding time to return items. Many stores now have stricter return policies and very short windows for returns and generally make it difficult to do so. Furthermore, several stores now track the number of returns you make and flag frequent returnees.

Budget Fashionista Secret #7: Become a Global Budget Shopper

According to my closest friends, I'm the real-life version of Rebecca Bloomwood, the main character in Sophie Kinsella's *Shopaholic* series of books, who ignores common sense and international laws to score deals. Unlike the *Shopaholic* character, I am usually broke when traveling, so I have to use creative means to get the best deals. One time I almost got thrown into jail while living in Ghana, West Africa, for bringing into the country ten yards of wax print fabric and three fabulous brass bracelets I purchased for $5 on a trip to Côte d'Ivoire (Ivory Coast). Another time I skipped out of a conference in India and spent five hours in a small New Delhi boutique negotiating the purchase of high-quality red silk fabric for my entire bridal party (twelve dresses) for $125.

In addition to these purchases, some of my best shopping deals were found during my global travels:

South Africa: a pair of Alexander McQueen–striped trousers for $15
Holland: Esprit cotton cardigan sweater for $23
Spain: black skirt with a red dragon from the Spanish store Zara for $6
Toronto: leather monogrammed bag from Roots Canada, two years before the craze hit the United States, for $45
Ghana: Brass cuff bracelets for 10 cents
Jamaica: Beautiful Pucci-esque floor-length floral print sundress for $25

I've also found great deals at outlet malls around the world. Outlet-mall chains like Chelsea's Premium Outlets (www.premium-outlets.com) have outlets in Japan and even a mall in Mexico City that house outlets of ultra-exclusive designers such as Lanvin and

Dolce & Gabbana. If you're heading to Europe, visit one of the thirteen MacArthurGlen Outlets (www.macarthurglen.com) or visit the outlets of designers Bally and Etro outside Florence, Italy. Legend has it that there is a Louis Vuitton outlet secretly located somewhere in Japan that only a few well-connected Japanese fashionistas know about. For more information about outlet malls outside the United States, visit TheBudgetFashionista.com.

The Budget Fashionista Explains:
What Is a VAT?

A VAT (Value Added Tax) is a general tax levied on goods and services by the government of a country. All European Union countries have a VAT of at least 15 percent, and several other countries have their own version of a VAT. Although refundable for nonresidents, it is still annoying because getting a VAT refund can be a major hassle. You should inquire about the refund procedures at the time of purchase. Sometimes you can avoid the hassle altogether by having your purchases shipped back to the United States.

These are just a few of my shopping secrets. If you have one that you'd like to share, please feel free to shoot an e-mail to tips@the-budgetfashionista.com. I'm always looking for new secrets and tips to add to my bargain bag.

Chapter 12

The Big Guns: Department Stores

Department stores—mammoth retail establishments divided into several sections or departments—are a necessary evil for budget fashionistas because we often find our best deals at these stores. Department stores tend to focus less on the trendy (they have special departments for these items) and more on what will consistently sell, making them a great place to find staple pieces such as a good black suit or a pair of jeans.

Scoring Coupons for Your Favorite Department Stores

Finding coupons for department stores can be as simple as turning on your computer. The easiest way to get these coupons is visit the store's website and search using the term *coupon* or ask a salesperson when shopping how you can get on the store's preferred customer list. Lord & Taylor, the venerable department store located throughout the East Coast and Midwest, frequently has coupons available on its site for you to print out. They will also send notifications of their latest coupons via their e-mail newsletter. Off 5th, Saks Fifth Avenue's outlet store, and Last Call Neiman Marcus liberally send out coupons that offer an extra 25 percent off to customers on their mailing list. The shoe mecca DSW regularly sends out coupons to customers on their preferred customer list. Bloomingdale's and Macy's both offer coupons, sometimes only to store credit card holders, but I've received coupons as a non–card holder as well. But be sure to visit the stores' websites for more details.

Select List of Department Stores with E-commerce Sites	
Store	**Website**
Bloomingdale's	www.bloomingdales.com
Boscov's	www.boscovs.com
Dillard's	www.dillards.com
Filene's	www.filenes.com
Lord & Taylor	www.lordandtaylor.com
Macy's	www.macys.com
Neiman Marcus	www.neimanmarcus.com
Nordstrom	www.nordstrom.com
Saks Fifth Avenue	www.saksfifthavenue.com
Sears	www.sears.com
Strawbridge's	www.strawbridges.com

There seems to be an adversarial relationship developing between shoppers and the sales associates at their favorite stores. While in many cases customer service has suffered a bit, becoming friends with the sales associates at your favorite store is still the best way to learn about the best deals. They have insider information on the latest sales and new shipments, and may have coupons and other discounts available to give to customers. Sales associates, especially in non-commission-based stores, are often paid not much more than minimum wage, so there is no incentive for them to go that extra mile and head to the massive backroom. Being a friendly face, giving positive feedback for good service, hanging up your clothes and returning them to the sales associate after trying them on, and even offering to buy her/him coffee or lunch can go a long way toward establishing a relationship with a sales associate. Being nice can get you better service and save you money.

Budget Fashionista Tip #24: The Best Times of Year to Shop

The best time of year to shop depends on your personal style and your closet needs. The best time to shop for classic items for your Perfect Ten is during the off-season (fall and winter months for spring and summer items, and spring and summer months for fall and winter items). If you want an item that's a trend without paying top dollar, then go to an end-of-season sale (generally in August for summer items, November for fall items, February for winter items, and May for spring items). During these sales, retailers try to move the old season's merchandise out of the store in order to free up precious retail space for the incoming season, and usually whatever trend was hot that season is left over in abundance. In addition, many stores have big sales for major holidays such as the Fourth of July, Presidents' Day, and Labor Day.

Inside Scoop: Carol Davidson, Former Manager at Macy's By Appointment—Personal Shopping Services and Certified Image Consultant

Carol Davidson is the Obi-Wan Kenobi of shopping—using her budget wisdom and style advice to help people improve their personal image via her image consulting business, StyleWorks of Union Square. This former director of corporate sales at Zagat (the restaurant guide people) and former manager of Personal Shopping Services at the world's largest department store, Macy's in Herald Square, is also an instructor at New York's Fashion Institute of Technology's image consulting program. Carol sat down between appointments with shopping clients to give us the scoop on how to find bargains at your local department store.

What's a personal shopper?

Personal shoppers are employees of the store who are there to help you find (and, of course, buy) clothes. Many of the major department stores, including Macy's, Bloomingdale's, Saks Fifth Avenue, Marshall Field's, and Nordstrom, have a personal shopping service available at no cost to customers. These services are often located in a special section of the store and have goodies like complimentary beverages, courtesy phone, and bigger, more appointed fitting rooms with no garment maximums. Although there is no minimum purchase required to use the service, be aware that some personal shoppers get paid by commission.

What's the best time to shop at a department store?

Monday mornings are great because few people shop at the beginning of the week. Another good time is a half hour before closing.

When do markdowns usually take place?

First, let's clarify the difference between a markdown and a sale. A markdown implies that the item will stay at that price; a sale indicates that the store can bring the price up to full retail. The time frame for markdowns varies from store to store, but usually it's about eight weeks after the item arrives on the floor. Some department stores such as Macy's have a higher volume so items are marked down more quickly.

As the former manager of personal shopping at a major department store, you must have developed some great shopping tips. What are some of your secret "insider" shopping tips?

A great tip is that most department stores have coupons available in their visitor center. Sometimes they don't ask for any ID, so you can ask for a coupon even though you may not be a visitor but live near the store. Also, if you visit cities like New York and Los Angeles, you can avoid paying sales tax by having the clothes shipped back home. Some stores will even ship your purchases for free. In addition, in many stores, such as Saks Fifth Avenue, when you purchase an item at full price, you can request free alterations. Furthermore, the store's personal shoppers have look books of all the lines they carry and can help you find other pieces from the line of your favorite designer, regardless of whether they are carried in their stores.

The Budget Fashionista Explains:
How to Shop During the Holidays

As a budget fashionista you must know how to
shop during the media-frenzied, retail-orgy time
called the holiday season. Most of us would agree
that the holidays have become as commercialized as
good old Saint Nick himself. You barely have enough time to remove your Halloween costume before there is an onslaught of com-
mercials for Christmas (and Hanukkah and Kwanzaa and Ramadan
and Diwali). So how does one survive this holiday gift-giving season
with style and sanity? Follow these tips:

Shop between February and September. I start my holiday shopping in early March, at the tail end of the winter sales. This is a
particularly good time to obtain stocking stuffers or smaller nonsea-
sonal items like bath and beauty products. As an example, I found
several 100 percent cashmere sweaters for men at Off 5th, Saks Fifth
Avenue Outlet for 70 percent off; they were $28 each. Granted, it
was April, but the men in my family didn't care when they saw their
Saks Fifth Avenue cashmere sweaters.

Shop the day after Christmas. This is a great trick if you aren't near
your family during the holidays. Purchase your gifts on December
26 and send them to family members via USPS Priority Mail
(which, strangely, sometimes costs the same as regular ground). You
save a bundle, and they get more presents to open.

Theme gift giving. This tip saves you not only time but money as
well. For example, I like to give an item like cool socks to all the fel-
las on my list and earrings to all the women. Everyone needs a pair
of socks, and socks are fairly cheap. Some other great theme gifts are
beauty and bath products, gloves, hats, scarves, and cool T-shirts.

Make it. Making gifts can be a cheap alternative to purchasing gifts.
If you love to cook, hand out gift certificates for a free dinner. Trust
me, any busy family on your list will love that gift.

Donate to charity. The best gift for those who have everything is to give to someone else. Send a donation in their name to groups like UNICEF, American Cancer Society, Greenpeace, or even their political party.

Give them what they want. Don't waste your money on something they won't wear. As a budget fashionista you hate bad gifts, so don't be a bad gift giver. Also, you don't want to be embarrassed if they have to return the item and find out you paid only $5 for the Prada bag.

Off-Price Department Stores

Off-price department stores are some of the best places to get previous and current seasonal overstocks from major designers. The quality of the merchandise varies according to location. For example, the T.J. Maxx in St. Louis Park, Minnesota, is vastly different from the T.J. Maxx in Dallas, Texas. The Loehmann's in suburban Philadelphia, Pennsylvania, is very different from Loehmann's in Beverly Hills, California.

Top Off-Price Department Stores		
Store	**Location**	**Specialty**
Century 21 (www.c21store.com)	New York metropolitan area	A favorite of New York budget fashionistas; known for major deals on high-end and couture designers like Dior and Chanel. Also has housewares and children's clothing. Avoid like the plague on the weekends.

Store	Location	Specialty
Daffy's (www.daffys.com)	New York metropolitan area, Philadelphia	Has one of the best lingerie departments.
Filene's Basement (www.filenesbasement .com)	Georgia, Illinois, Ohio, East Coast	The nation's oldest off-price store; known for its annual bridal sales.
K&G (www.kgmens.com)	Nationwide	Known mostly for their discounted men's fashions, particularly suits. Several of these superstores carry a large selection of lower-quality women's suits.
Loehmann's (www.loehmanns .com)	Arizona, California, Colorado, Florida, Georgia, Illinois, Texas, Washington, the East Coast	Known for their back room; carries merchandise from high-end designers like St. John Knits, Moschino, and Prada for a fraction of the price. Sign up for their preferred shoppers club and receive coupons for an additional percentage off.
Marshalls (www .marshallsonline .com)	Nationwide	A favorite of budget fashionistas nationwide
Ross (www.rossstores.com)	West Coast, Mid-Atlantic, the South	Has an excellent selection of household items including furniture.

Store	Location	Specialty
Syms (www.syms.com)	37 stores nationwide	A wide selection of designer fashions for men, women, and children. Sign up for newsletter and receive an additional 10 percent off.
T.J. Maxx (www.tjmaxx.com)	Nationwide	Owned by the same company as Marshalls; has an excellent accessory department

The Budget Fashionista's $50 Challenge

One beautiful Saturday afternoon my friend Kevin and I set out on a mission to find a stylish outfit for me to wear to my friend Sira's birthday party for less than $50. With little time and a small amount of money, we headed to a local strip mall. Kevin, who has worked with Diane von Furstenberg, Faconnable, and Kenneth Cole, suggested we stop at the new Marshalls that had opened up not too far from our northern New Jersey homes. I agreed.

When shopping under a rather extreme budget and looking for an outfit for an event, I focus on finding a key piece and then building the rest of the outfit around it. For events like birthday parties, formal dinners, and so forth, where most of the attention will be on the upper half of your body, focus on purchasing killer tops and accessories such as a great necklace and cool earrings.

On the lookout for a great top, we headed straight for the misses' clearance rack and found a kelly green T-shirt from Polo Ralph Lauren for $16.99. I was a little apprehensive about the shirt because I'm not a big fan of ornate graphics, but Kevin convinced me that it was a great top and an excellent color to complement my skin. When shopping on a strict budget, don't be afraid to try new pieces. It's often out of the desperation brought on by a fashion crisis that you find new items to add to your favorites list. I begrudgingly put the shirt in the basket.

The ultimate find of the day was a cream-colored, delicately cro-cheted, bat-winged cardigan sweater. I loved this sweater because it would work well with several pieces in my closet, and it was cheap ($17.99). Kevin noticed that it was in the same color family as the print on the kelly green T-shirt and suggested I try wearing the cardi-gan over the shirt. The key to mixing and matching styles and trends is to find a common theme between the pieces. It can be a color (as in my case) or a similar fabric (cotton sweater with linen pants) or similar fabric weight (velvet with brocade).

We had the T-shirt and the lace cardigan, but we had no bottom. With only $15 left in our budget, there was only one place for us to go: Wal-Mart. According to Kevin, jeans from the Faded Glory line at this mass-market retailer are some of the best in terms of fit, and they usually retail for around $15, perfect for our budget. After mak-ing our purchases at Marshalls and waiting in the long checkout line (apparently a fellow shopper had slipped on a hamburger in the misses' pants aisle), we headed over to Wal-Mart to purchase the jeans.

On my site I usually tell readers never to go to a Wal-Mart or Tar-get on a Saturday. I didn't follow my own advice. Everyone in New Jersey was in the store on that Saturday. Lucky for us, the misses' sec-tion was located near the front of the store. We went over to the Faded Glory jeans and found a pair for $14.92. Total cost of outfit: $51.40 including tax.

How to Navigate Messy and Unorganized Stores

Although great deals can be found at off-price stores like Marshalls, the stores are often messy and unorganized. As an expert budget shopper, I've perfected the art of navigating these stores and can offer you these tips:

1. Go on a weekday before 11 A.M. It is usually quieter and cleaner because the store has just opened.
2. Have a clear goal in mind. Knowing what you are looking for will save you time.

3. Eat before entering the store and carry a bottle of water. Discount department stores are notorious for their high temperatures.
4. Look for alternative locations. Try heading to the downtown location of your favorite stores during the weekend or the suburban location on a weekday morning.
5. If possible, don't carry a purse, hat, or any other accessory that you care about. It will just get in the way, and there is a chance you will lose it.

Mass-Market Discount Stores

It used to be that mass-market discount stores like Kmart and Wal-Mart, were places where trends went to die. Then entered Target. Target revolutionized the mass-market industry by introducing such high-end designers as Isaac Mizrahi and Cynthia Rowley to the masses and demonstrating that coolness has no geographical or economic boundaries. Now top fashion stylists and editors head to stores like Target and Kohl's to find great pieces for high/low dressing. Don't be afraid to mix a silk sweater purchased at Wal-Mart with that Cynthia Steffe sundress you purchased at Saks, or pair a Dolce & Gabbana top with a pair of Levi Signature jeans from Target.

The Budget Fashionista Explains: Mass-Market Discount Store Lines for High/Low Dressing

Wal-Mart (www.walmart.com). The George line offers many fashion-forward items for the budget fashionista on an extreme budget.

Kmart (www.kmart.com). There is more to Kmart than Martha Stewart. Look for pieces from its Route 66 denim line and international superstar Thalia Sodi's hip line.

Kohl's (www.kohls.com). Recently Kohl's has started to emerge as a fashion force for those who are intimidated by Target's youth-focused styles. The store carries lines from Daisy Fuentes, Nine & Company, Levi's, and the reemerging Gloria Vanderbilt.

Target (www.target.com). The Isaac Mizrahi line continues to wow both fashionistas and style novices alike. Don't overlook the Mossimo line, however; it produces its own inspired versions of the latest trends.

Again, fit is extremely important when assessing what to purchase from a discount store. If the item doesn't fit you well, it will make the entire outfit, including the expensive item, look cheap. Shop these stores like you would shop an expensive designer boutique.

Chapter 13

Shopping Centers and Outlet Malls

From the Mall of America to your local strip mall, shopping centers and malls are most Americans' primary source for shopping. Since there are more than 45,000 shopping centers in the United States today,* they are as much a part of our lives as parking tickets and designer coffee.

For budget fashionistas who live outside big cities, it can be a challenge to find fashionable clothing at the local mall. The hard truth is that most malls feature the same basic stores (the Gap, The Limited, Victoria's Secret, etc.), making it difficult to be original. Use these tricks to create fashionable outfits from your local resources.

1. **Find a centerpiece.** Search your mall for a distinct or unusual piece and build your entire outfit around that piece. This piece could be a great top, bottom, bag, purse, whatever, as long as it is unusual and a conversation starter. You don't necessarily have to spend a bundle on this item.
2. **Fit over fashion.** Most mall items are mass-produced, which sometimes means that the quality and fit are compromised. Make sure the garment fits you and, if necessary, bring it to your local tailor.

---

* This information is from the International Council of Shopping Centers, http://www.icsc.org/srch/rsrch/scope/current/index.shtml, August 1, 2005.

3. **Designer-inspired replicas.** Take your look book into stores to help you find items that look like pieces from your favorite designers. Since most mall-based stores focus on trends that have reached mass-market saturation, your look book will help you focus on finding "the next big thing" before it reaches everyone. Review "Starting Your Own Trends" (page 120) for more guidance.

4. **Hit *every* department.** Just because you're a senior doesn't mean you can't hit the juniors' department, and young fashionistas can find great items in the misses' department. For example, I was participating in a shopping contest sponsored by the Style Network at a local mall in Chattanooga, Tennessee, and found a deep-purple velvet blazer on sale for $18 in the "granny" section of the misses' department.

Top Mall Stores

Ashley Stewart (www.ashleystewart.com). This store is a muumuu-free zone for stylish plus-size fashionistas who want to be trendy. Budget fashionistas of all sizes will appreciate the amazing costume jewelry selection, with most pieces well under $15.

Ann Taylor (www.anntaylor.com). I wouldn't necessarily call Ann Taylor "budget," but if you're in a pinch, Ann Taylor is a great store to find a nice pair of dress slacks or a quick outfit for that important meeting. I always head straight to the back of the store to the clearance rack to search for mid-priced deals on basics. Remember, it's okay to spend a little more on your Perfect Ten, and Ann Taylor is one of the best places to find them.

Bebe (www.bebe.com). I rarely shop at Bebe, but members of my budget advisory board swear by this mall "boutique." Think of it as South Beach meets your local PTA. Look for their butt-enhancing jeans.

Charlotte Russe (www.charlotterusse.com). This store is my guilty pleasure. Less manic than Forever 21 and better stocked than Wet Seal, Charlotte Russe has all the latest trends for well under $30.

Older fashionistas will appreciate the large accessories section, which will allow you to add hip pieces into your wardrobe without looking like a teenage wannabe.

The Gap (www.gap.com). I will always love the Gap, no matter how much they may stray from their denim roots. The Gap is still one of the best places in the mall to find jeans and T-shirts in normal people sizes (up to XXL in tops and size 18 in jeans) and normal people price ranges. The best deals in the store are actually in the back room; always ask a sales associate to look in back for a size or style. Also, always ask if there is a friends and family coupon that you can use.

H&M (www.hm.com). I like to think that if I had a billion dollars and could develop my own store, it would be just like H&M, with designer-inspired pieces copied right off the Fashion Week runways at amazing prices. The quality can be hit or miss and selection varies from mall to mall, but for the most part the store is a great place to get right-now looks, well, right now. If your mall has an H&M, there is absolutely no reason to purchase high-end costume jewelry from expensive department stores.

Talbots (www.talbots.com). Once, in a desperate attempt to find some "television-ready" outfits for less than the cost of my college education, I headed to my local mall. After hitting all the usual places and finding absolutely nothing, I headed to Talbots. Now, I wouldn't describe the store as trendy or hip or, at $150 for a dress, cheap, *but* it's worth taking a peek at their sales racks.

Be sure to utilize the tailoring services at your favorite mall stores. Stores such as Banana Republic and J. Crew offer free alterations on full-price items. Even though I rarely pay full price for an item, when I do, I utilize these services to ensure a perfect fit.

Shopping in Action

My friend Monique had been buried deep in the fluorescent-lighted recesses of a hospital for three years, finishing a residency in orthopedic surgery, when she called me needing urgent closet surgery. It is not as if Monique doesn't have style—she actually has quite a bit—but her style is more suited to the warm tropical climate of her native Jamaica than the harsh winters of Connecticut, and examining patients in a pair of flip-flops and a flower-printed skirt just wouldn't work.

So I hopped on Amtrak and headed to my alma mater to visit my dear friend. When I arrived in New Haven, we assessed her budget; by some brilliant banking maneuvers, Monique was able to gather $600 for this new wardrobe, which was the equivalent of her entire clothing budget for the year. She needed a wardrobe that would last her until May 2007, the end of her residency, and her personal style tended to fall more toward the conservative end of the spectrum. Our shopping strategy, therefore, was to focus more on quality than quantity.

This was our shopping list:

- bras and underwear (in the right sizes!)
- layering tops (great for wearing under suit jackets, sweaters, and other T-shirts)
- black velvet suit jacket (very sexy and slimming)
- basic black dress (remember the Perfect Ten)
- one pair of simple earrings (something basic that could be worn professionally)
- collared dress shirts (classic and never go out of style)
- pants (black, gray, brown)
- shoes (black boots, black heels)
- one fun item or shirt (a girl has to have some fun)

We set out in Monique's 1989 Nissan/Toyota/Hyundai (it was so old that the make no longer mattered) to Westfarm Mall in central Connecticut. I chose this mall because we needed to find some basic pieces, and Westfarm has a wide variety of great department stores. Plus, it was the best mall within the very limited travel distance of her car.

When we got to the mall, Nordstrom was winding down their semiannual women's and children's sale with savings of an additional 30 to 50 percent off regular price, so we headed there first. Nordstrom is an excellent place to pick up high-quality basic pieces.

We found a pair of black Ralph Lauren (green label) pants on sale and had them tailored for $83.63. I persuaded Monique to spend a little more on these than she'd expected to because they were lined, increasing the wear of the garment, and the tailoring would ensure a perfect fit. This is one of the pluses to shopping at a department store; they often have tailors on staff to help you fit the pants to your body. We also picked up a pair of black suede pumps and knee-high black boots for approximately $40 apiece.

Total at Nordstrom: $163.63

The next item to find was some basic high-quality stretchy T-shirts. The best place to find these tees, hands down, is Old Navy. Yes, other places carry them, but Old Navy's Perfect Fit T-shirts are similar in quality to the more expensive brands and usually cost less than $12. Unfortunately, this mall did not have an Old Navy, so we headed to the Gap. (For a budget fashionista, it's important to know the style twins of your favorite stores, so if your favorite store doesn't have what you're looking for, you will know other stores that carry similar items.) At the Gap we found four layering T-shirts (in black, white, pink, and purple) for about the same price as Old Navy.

Total at the Gap: $49.93

Next we headed to Lord & Taylor, one of my favorite shopping haunts. Monique tried on several pairs of pants, but nothing seemed to work, mostly because she was wearing the wrong undergarments. It is important to wear *good* underwear when you go shopping because it will affect the look of the garment you're trying on. We didn't let poor undergarments disrupt our flow: Monique bought a nice black Ralph Lauren cotton dress blouse and a pair of "diamond" earrings. We figured she would be able to replace them with real ones after her residency.

Total at Lord & Taylor: $49.18

Propelled to action by the sad state of her underwear, we headed straight to the intimates section of Filene's department store. Now, I really truly love Monique, but I am *never* going undergarment shopping with her again. First, we had an argument over the tank top bra issue. She said they were comfortable (they are). I said they give women a "uniboob" (they do). After spending fifteen minutes arguing, during which she threatened to strangle me with a padded demi-bra, we reached a compromise: She got the tank top bra thing but listened to my pleas to purchase several pairs of sensible underwear with a little nylon to help uplift and hold in her "goods."

After leaving the intimates section, we headed to the women's department, where we proceeded to wrap up the shopping. We found a great white cotton dress shirt, a pair of brown slacks, and a black knit top from MICHAEL by Michael Kors (his latest bridge line), a pair of gray tweed pants from Ralph Lauren, and a beautiful kelly green suede jacket from Inc. We also found a great black dress, but Monique felt she wouldn't wear it until summer. Flashing back to my near-death experience with the padded demi-bra, I decided not to push the dress any further.

Total at Filene's: $313

At the end of our trip, this is what we'd purchased:

- two bras and six pairs of underwear
- four layering tops
- one pair of "diamond" earrings
- two dress shirts (white, black)
- one black sweater
- three pairs of high-quality slacks (black, brown, gray)
- one pair of black pumps
- one pair of black boots
- one buttery soft green suede jacket

The total spent was $575.74 for a completely new head-to-toe professional wardrobe with designer items and tailoring. Time spent with one of my best friends: priceless.

Outlet Malls: The Holiday Inns of the Millennium

Road trips are the quintessential summer adventure. When I was a kid, my family would pile into the Chevy Cavalier and drive to exciting places like Topeka, Kansas, and Jonesboro, Arkansas. No matter where we were going, there was always a Holiday Inn at the next exit. Twenty years later it seems that Holiday Inns have been replaced by outlet malls.

Take a road trip to any part of the United States, and I guarantee that you will drive past at least one outlet mall. Between Exit 6 (Pennsylvania Turnpike) and Exit 18 (George Washington Bridge) on the New Jersey Turnpike there are at least four outlet malls, including the mammoth Jersey Garden Mall. Signs for outlet malls are sprinkled up and down Interstate 95. Even Medford, Minnesota, population 788, has an outlet mall.

Retailers have finally figured out what budget fashionistas have known for years: When we are bored, we like to shop, and what could possibly be more boring than a nineteen-hour trip from Minneapolis, Minnesota, to Jonesboro, Arkansas, in a Ford Taurus? Although the quality of outlet malls varied from interstate to interstate, they were a welcome alternative to urine-smelling rest stops and counting roadkill.

Budget Fashionista Tip #25: Get a Coupon Book

Don't even think about shopping at an outlet mall without first obtaining one of their coupon books. These books, usually found at the visitor or information kiosks, have tons of coupons for additional discounts or free gifts with purchase. Try to get a coupon book for free by going online to the outlet's website and printing out a request for a free coupon book. If you forget this step, just head to the visitor or information kiosks and tell them you came in on a tour bus from (choose any town) and didn't get a coupon book.

Shopping at outlet malls is a tricky activity. Sometimes you can hit the jackpot, and other times it would have been better to stay home. Some outlets carry "special" lines at their outlet stores that are really products of lesser quality than those sold in the main stores.

The Budget Fashionista Explains: Definition of a Good Outlet Store

Some outlet stores are not really outlet stores. They use that term to sucker budget-conscious folks like us into purchasing items that are of inferior quality and still overpriced. Here are the guidelines I use in determining a good outlet store.

- Prices are at least 30 percent below the manufacturer's suggested retail price (MSRP). Many stores add up to 20 percent and sometimes more to the MSRP. So a 20-percent-off sale is really selling the merchandise for its MSRP. Find out the MSRP by calling the designer's company or checking their website.
- The store has current or recent-season merchandise. I don't care if that pair of acid-wash jeans is only $4. If you're not going to wear them, you've wasted your money.
- The store should be a little messy. Budget shoppers are notoriously messy folks. If an outlet store is very neat, it is your first warning that the deals may not be very good.
- The merchandise must be of high quality and in good shape. Designers and stores often use their outlets to dump damaged and low-quality goods.

Fashionable Flashback: My Favorite Outlet Store

It was my mother who introduced me to Off 5th, Saks Fifth Avenue Outlet. A Saks Fifth Avenue was opening in downtown Minneapolis, and we had received an invitation to the opening. As we entered the store, an overwhelming feeling swept over me—the unexplainable connection you feel when for the first time in your life someone understands you and your needs. I was in love.

My mother, who would shop at Target even if she were a billionaire, led me to the fifth floor where the outlet store was located. Only in Minnesota would a high-end department store like Saks have its outlet store located on the top floor of the main store. As we approached, I could hear the hallelujah chorus in my head. Right next to the escalator was the handbag collection with these purses from a designer called Prada.

You see, for a budget fashionista who was living outside New York City before the Internet leveled the shopping playing field, it was almost impossible to find designer clothes. Budget fashionistas in the middle states were stuck with whatever the buyers at their local department store would purchase, which for those of us in the upper Midwest *meant jeans and sweats. There was little or no hope for fashionistas like myself who, despite geographical location, were still stylistas. Finding the Prada purses at a discount was nothing short of a miracle. To say that Off 5th influenced my dressing is an understatement. My black Calvin Klein cashmere coat, purchased from the outlet for $90, was a major fixture in my college wardrobe. I wore my pair of Yves Saint Laurent sandals, purchased for $26, every day during the summer of 1994.*

One of the best deals I ever found was a Tom and Linda Platt evening dress, à la Oleg Cassini 1962, for $75 (originally about $1,500, it was marked down to $375 plus 75 percent off and a coupon for 25 percent off). Another time I bought five cashmere sweaters for $80 at the outlet. Even the cashier couldn't believe my finds and called over two of her coworkers to see the deals I was able to purchase.

Budget Fashionista Tip #26: Join the VIP Club

Some outlet malls, like those owned by Chelsea Premium Outlets (for instance, Woodbury Commons in upstate New York), have a VIP club that offers special deals and coupons to their members. The catch is that you need to register an e-mail address. These coupons are not available in the regular coupon book, so if you're planning a major shopping day, it's worth it to sign up for the newsletter. Create a special shopping e-mail account on Yahoo! or Hotmail to use for all your shopping newsletters, coupon offers, and so forth. This will help you keep track of the deals as well as keep your e-mail clear of spam.

My Favorite Outlet Stores

Bottega Veneta (www.bottegaveneta.com). Get this high-end Italian designer at prices you can actually afford.

Burberry (www.burberry.com). Acquire the famous trench coats and accessories for a fraction of the retail price.

Coach (www.coach.com). This outlet is one of the few places to find pieces from the original classic line of leather goods. Head there during the change of seasons for great deals.

Donna Karan (www.donnakaran.com). There is always a sale at this outlet store that features items for both men and women.

Ellen Tracy (www.ellentracy.com). Offers classic career wear, including plus sizes and petites. Make sure you ask about the friends and family coupon.

Ferragamo (www.ferragamo.com). Shoes, accessories, and other leather goods from the top shoe manufacturer are at reasonable prices—including current season merchandise.

Last Call Neiman Marcus. Has better deals on St. John Knits, Armani, and other big designers than the designers' own outlet stores. Make sure you check out this outlet's collection of designer bridal gowns that are from 30 percent off the retail price and sign up for e-mail alerts.

Off 5th, Saks Fifth Avenue Outlet. This is the outlet store of the designer mecca. Look for the colored dot on the tags to save even more money.

St. John Knits (www.st.johnknits.com). This exclusive knit company's outlet is where you can find a $1,000 jacket for $250. There are only a few of them nationwide, but if you are a follower of this knit company, make sure you note the locations of these shops.

Via Spiga (www.viaspiga.com). Shoes from the footwear designer are sold at significantly reduced prices. The outlet carries up to a size 11 in women's shoes and a good selection of shoes for men.

Top Outlet Malls

Atlanta: **Discover Mills** (www.discovermills.com). Find major designer discounts at this outlet. The mall houses the outlets of

Neiman Marcus, Levi, Saks Fifth Avenue, and more. Also check out the North Georgia Premium Outlets.

Chicago: **Gurnee Mills Mall** (**www.gurneemillsmall.com**). This was the first outlet mall I ever visited. It has something for fashionistas of all ages: an Abercrombie & Fitch outlet for the young and a Chico outlet for the more mature. Visit the website to sign up for special deals.

Houston: **Katy Mills Mall** (**www.katymillsmall.com**). Go to the Galleria to find the styles, but head to Katy Mills to buy them. This outlet mall is part of the Mills outlet mall chain. Off 5th, Saks Fifth Avenue Outlet is *the* place to head for major discounts on top designers such as Chloe, Prada, St. John, Ellen Tracy, Dana Buchman, and more.

Las Vegas: **Fashion Outlets of Las Vegas** (**www.fashionoutletlasvegas.com**). There are several outlet malls located in the Las Vegas area, but this is the best. Located right outside the Strip, this mall offers shoppers up to 75 percent off fashions from Burberry, Escada, Tahari, Versace, and others. Definitely check with one of the hotels on the Strip or at the mall's website for coupons and special offers.

Maine: **Freeport** (**www.freeportusa.com**). This little seacoast village houses more than 170 outlet shops, including the outdoor favorite L.L. Bean. Be sure to wear comfortable shoes because the outlets are spread throughout the town.

Minnesota: **Albertville Premium Outlets** (**www.premiumoutlets.com**). Located about an hour outside of Minneapolis, this is the best outlet mall in the Twin Cities metropolitan area. You'll find the outlets of Jones New York, Tommy Hilfiger, and Wilson's Leather.

New York: **Woodbury Commons** (**www.premiumoutlets.com**). This is the mother of all outlet malls. Located about an hour outside New York City, it's home to Chanel, Burberry, and Bottega Veneta outlets all in one mall. Fashionistas flock to this outlet when they want to score high-priced items at up to 80 percent off the retail price. During the summer and early fall the outlets can be beyond packed—my advice is to head there right before the change of seasons—late February/early March for great fall deals and late July/ early August for great spring and summer deals. The mall is open-air, so be sure to dress as warm as possible in the winter.

Philadelphia: **Franklin Mills (www.franklinmills.com).** Right outside the city. Most of the mall is not up to par, but great deals can be found at Off 5th, Saks Fifth Avenue Outlet, Last Call Neiman Marcus, and a Marshalls superstore.

Fort Lauderdale/Miami: **Saw Grass Mills (www.sawgrassmills .com).** Part of the Mills outlet chain, this one has some great department store outlets such as Last Call Neiman Marcus and outlets of top designers such as St. John Knits.

St. Louis: **St. Louis Mills Outlet Center (www.stlouismills.com).** One of the newest members of the Mills group of outlet malls, this one houses some of the most fashion-forward stores in the Midwest. Find clothing from Juicy Couture, Dior, Prada, and more at the Off 5th, Saks Fifth Avenue Outlet.

Toronto: **Dixie Outlet Mall (www.dixieoutletmall.com).** This is one of the best outlet malls in the Toronto area. You'll find great savings on deals from Canadian favorites such as Tabi, Winners, and Jacob. Stop by the visitor center to obtain a coupon book.

Do you have a favorite outlet store or mall that you want to share? Please e-mail me at info@thebudgetfashionista.com.

Chapter 14

Sample Sales and Warehouse Sales

The traditional definition of a sample sale is an event where a designer, design house, or store sells its "sample" merchandise. This includes the items created to promote the designer's line in fashion shows, in showings to store buyers, and for use in photo spreads for magazines. Traditionally, sample sales are limited to clothing sizes 4 to 6 and size 7 in shoes, which excludes pretty much everyone except Naomi Campbell. However, many have expanded their sales to include other sizes as well. Discounts can range from 20 percent to 80 percent off retail.

There is no set rule for who gets in or how many people get into a sample sale. It really depends on the designer or store having the sample sale and the limits of the space. Usually, once you are in the sale, you can stay as long as you like; however, many places regulate the number of people who are let into a sale. Unless you have a connection or a special pass, there is no way to know if you will get into the sale. Examples of great sample sales are Chanel's and Prada's annual sales. The best sample sales are held in larger cities that have large fashion communities, including New York, Los Angeles, and London.

On the other end of the spectrum are warehouse sales. These are usually major sales of overstocked items from current or past seasons by a designer (as in the case of the St. John Knits warehouse sale) or a store (as in the case of the Barneys warehouse sale). Whereas sample sales tend to sell only limited sizes (think models), warehouse sales tend to have a larger variety of sizes and styles. For example, many designers, like Lily Pulitzer, hold major warehouse sales.

Sample sales and warehouse sales are different from department store sales which also clear out space for new merchandise and sell leftovers from previous seasons. The big difference is that department store sales usually have a bigger selection of merchandise and sizes than the other sales.

Every budget fashionista must attend at least one sample sale in her lifetime, if only to see how unbridled consumerism can turn normally sane and stable people into rabid shoppers willing to wait three hours in a downpour to purchase a $200 bag from two seasons ago. The lines at popular sample sale events, such as the Kate Spade sale in New York City, sometimes wrap around the block two times or three times—all of this for merchandise you can get at Off 5th, Saks Fifth Avenue Outlet any day of the week. My advice is to go to the sample sale, and if there is a long line, head right to the nearest Loehmann's, Nordstrom Rack, Off 5th, Saks Fifth Avenue Outlet, and/or Last Call Neiman Marcus.

The term *sample sale* invokes such a reaction from fashionistas that it seems as though every publicist and event promoter is using the term whether or not the event they are promoting is actually a sample sale. To be perfectly honest, most sample sales are overrated. There is usually a limited amount of each item, the products are often damaged or a color you couldn't possibly wear (puke green), and the place is almost always a mess. However, you can find some incredible deals at these sample sales, such as classic coats, designer handbags, and even designer wedding dresses.

Visit TheBudgetFashionista.com for up-to-date information on sample sales and other sales events around the United States and Canada.

Budget Fashionista Tip #27: Five Things *Not* to Bring to a Sample Sale

1. **Your three-year-old.** Most samples sales don't allow children younger than twelve into the sale.

2. **A big coat.** Once inside, the room temperature at sample sales is so hot that you could start to see mirages of Evian. If possible, leave your coat at home.

3. **Arthritis.** Samples sales can be as brutal as an Australian rugby game. If you have "Arthur," lather up with Ben-Gay.

4. **Credit cards.** Credit cards are usually accepted, but it's much easier to just shell out the cash. Plus, it stops you from buying any crazy stuff.

5. **Shopping bags.** Most sample sales make you check your shopping bags at the door.

The Budget Fashionista's Best
Warehouse Sales, Sample Sales, and Sale Events

Atlanta: **Luxe Sale Events.** This Atlanta boutique (at 5,600 square feet it is more like a mini department store) holds frequent sample sales of bags from Tods and Jimmy Choo, and vintage pieces from the likes of Pucci, for up to 80 percent off the retail price.

Southern California: **St. John Knits (www.stjohnknits.com).** This sale is so popular that they had to institute a wristband system in order to control traffic. Once a year the diva of knits opens the warehouse to a major sale with up to 60 percent off the retail price. Fans of the knit company swear by this sale.

New York City: **Kate Spade (held at Metropolitan Pavilion, www.metropolitanpavilion.com).** This is one of the most anticipated sample sale events in the city. Fashionistas form a line that extends around the block to purchase chic purses, shoes, and accessories from the queen of simple chic.

Philadelphia: **Lily Pulitzer** (www.lilypulitzer.com). Shoppers from as far away as Japan travel to this semiannual sample sale, held just outside of Philadelphia. The prices are reduced, but the merchandise is limited to hundreds of the same styles. If you are a big Lily fan, then this is the event for you.

Minneapolis: **Joan and Robb's Not So Secret Sale** (www.joanand-robb.com). This event, held at the Mall of America, is the brainchild of Joan Steffen of HGTV's *Decorating Cents* and home decorating guru Robb Whittlef. It features a well-edited collection of household items and furniture that will help you create a home befitting a budget fashionista.

Minneapolis: **Opitz Outlet** (www.opitzoutlet.com). Every day is a sample sale at this amazing Midwest find. My god-sister Phillis has scored the most amazing purchases at this outlet, including a Marc Jacobs Stella bag for $200.

Chicago: **Beta Sample Sale.** This event, first held in February 2005, aims to bring the sample sale culture to the Midwest. You'll find major discounts on designer clothing and accessories.

Los Angeles and New York: **Barneys Warehouse Sale** (www.barneys.com). You haven't attended a sales event until you've gone to a Barneys Warehouse Sale. Held on both coasts, there is no better place to see true shopping in action. I have bruises (literally) from the New York sales where a disgruntled fashionista once elbowed me in my ribs as I reached for a Miu Miu leather tote bag. But finding normally ridiculously priced items for somewhat affordable prices is well worth moments of pain.

San Francisco: **Fashion Co-op** (www.fashioncoop.com). Fashion Co-op holds frequent sample sale events in both San Francisco and Los Angeles. Head out to this sale to score major discounts on up-and-coming designers.

I'm always on the lookout for excellent sale events to add to my list of favorites. If there is a great sale event that you know of, feel free to visit TheBudgetFashionista.com and send me the info.

Budget Fashionista Tip #28: New York City Sample Sales

As rule of thumb, the best times to hit the sample sales in New York City are in May and late October/early November.

Big sale events may be great occasions to score designer stuff for less, but the ultimate deals can be found at your local thrift store and consignment shops, as you'll see in the next chapter.

Visit TheBudgetFashionista.com for the latest on New York City sample sales.

Chapter 15

Recycled Fashion: Thrift and Consignment Stores

I'm smitten.

Along with chocolate and boot-cut jeans, I hereby declare my love for the Salvation Army thrift store. Sally's Boutique, as I affectionately call this thrift store giant, is a major part of my budget-shopping arsenal. One of my favorite childhood memories involves rummaging through the racks of the local Sally's with my seamstress grandma. It was our weekly ritual, and I never left the shop empty-handed. There was always a vintage patent-leather clutch or rhinestone brooch or Hermès-like silk scarf, with price tags well under $5.

Saks Fifth Avenue, my first love, has nothing on this store. Where else could you find a John Paul Gaultier shirt from Bergdorf Goodman for 99 cents? Or two vintage Norma Kamali dresses in perfect condition for $2.49 apiece. When I gave the two dresses to my friend Malinda, she was so excited that she started to shriek as though possessed by some strange budget-shopping demon. So fabulous were these dresses that she told me that sometimes she liked to wear them around her apartment. This is the power of the Salvation Army.

• • •

The Budget Fashionista Explains:
Five Things You MUST Know
Before Heading to the Thrift Store

1. **Buy what you like.** Shop at a thrift store as you would shop at a regular store: Only buy things that would normally interest you, and resist the urge to purchase items just because they're cheap.
2. **Conduct a smell test.** If it smells like armpits, leave it on the rack. Musty smells can be very difficult to remove.
3. **Wear form-fitting clothing.** Just in case the store doesn't have a fitting room.
4. **Bring cash.** Many thrift stores still don't have credit card machines.
5. **Shop in the rich areas.** The best thrift stores are located in wealthy areas. Wealthy people prefer the tax write-off they get from donating to the "little" money they get from consigning items.

Sally has provided relief for many of my fashion emergencies. For example, one weekend I needed a cocktail dress to wear to a business function. I found a beautiful black dress with black lace insets at the Salvation Army for $5. I added a silver leather belt from the Gap, a pair of silver flats from the Nine West Outlet, and a pair of silver square clip-on earrings from Nordstrom Rack—for a completely stunning outfit with a total cost of $48.

Before running out to your local Salvation Army or Goodwill, it is important to know a few key thrift store shopping tips. One tip is to make friends with the sales staff. Many people are so snotty toward the staff at the stores that they often miss out on the greatest finds. Roxanne, the manager at the Jersey City Salvation Army who helped me find great items, such as my short rabbit fur jacket circa 1968 for $16, is officially invited to my birthday party. She also helped me find a green vintage Coach purse for $9.99, scoring an invite for Thanksgiving dinner.

Another suggestion about shopping at the Salvation Army is to find out which color tag is on sale. Each week select stores place a different color tag on sale—usually 50 percent off. A knit dress I once found, originally from Bergdorf, was reduced from $6.99 to $3.50, less than the cost of a white chocolate mochaccino.

Again, make sure you shop the thrift store as you would a regular store. If it doesn't fit right, don't buy it. You don't want to end up with a closet full of items that will be returned to the store.

Here is how you can tell if an item at a thrift store is expensive:

- See if the tag uses a European sizing system (38, 42, etc.)
- Notice the designer (bring this book or a copy of the designer guide on my site)
- Check whether the garment is lined. Lining costs extra and can be a good indicator of the quality of the item.
- Look at the stitching. Is it even or crooked? Does it look as if someone took care in putting the item together?
- Judge it by its label. Does the label "look" expensive? Does it have the name of an expensive store?

The power of a thrift store extends past you and into the local community surrounding the store. Thrift stores help support the activities of the organization, which provide a wide range of social services to the community. You look fashionable while supporting your community. That is real shopping power.

Budget Fashionista Tip #29: Vintage Fashion Basics

Remember that sizes, like people, change over time. Sizes of clothing pre-1980 tend to run significantly smaller than comparable sizes today. The rule of thumb that I use is to add three or four sizes to your current size to find your vintage size; for example, if you wear a size 10 now, you would wear about a size 14 in vintage clothing. Also remember to pay attention to the care instructions. Because of age, vintage fabric tends to be much more delicate than that of newer items. Unless the label says otherwise, I send all vintage items to a reputable dry cleaner.

Some Other Great Thrift Stores

Goodwill (www.goodwill.org). Goodwill has a great selection of thrift goods, although the prices have risen considerably the past few years. Check out their online auction site.

Local hospital thrift stores. Many local hospitals have thrift stores run by their volunteer auxiliary. I find their prices a bit on the expensive side, but you can often find antique furniture for reasonable prices.

Junior Leagues. The Junior League is a social group of women committed to community service. The group is usually made up of older "established" women, so the thrift stores are mostly located in upscale areas, which means high-end goodies for budget fashionistas. The proceeds go toward helping to fund the organization's community service activities.

Local churches. Many churches operate thrift stores, and the type of merchandise carried at the store is related to the makeup of the congregation.

Budget Fashionista Tip #30: How to Clean Thrift Store Clothing

Never, ever wear a thrift store purchase without first cleaning the garment(s). If you can afford to, send the item to the cleaners. The fluid used to dry-clean items kills pretty much every germ imaginable. If the garment can't be dry-cleaned, then wash it once in the hottest water possible with a capful of a mild disinfectant and then a second time with a tablespoon of baking soda (to remove the disinfectant smell). Put it in the dryer at the highest possible heat. For shoes, jewelry, and other accessories, wipe the piece down with rubbing alcohol (test a small area to make sure it doesn't damage the piece) or spray with Lysol disinfectant spray.

Consignment Shops

Consignment shops, as you learned in Chapter 2, are places that sell high-quality secondhand (usually designer) clothing, shoes, and accessories in partnership with the owner of the clothing. Consignment shops are great places to look for gently used items from top designers. Consignment doesn't necessarily equate to budget, but the clothes are cheaper than buying them new at Barneys. Consignment shops are excellent places to score real designer goods for less. For example, at a great consignment shop like Ina's in New York, you might find pieces worn by Sarah Jessica Parker in *Sex and the City* for a fraction of their retail cost, or you can score used Hermès Birkin bags for $2,000, significantly less than the $6,000-plus price tag.

In some areas consignment shops are no better than your local thrift shop, but the ones that are well maintained and have well-selected merchandise can be like going to a fashion history class. Many shop owners are like fashion historians and are great sources when looking for a piece from a particular period or a particular style. Keep in mind that consignment shops aren't always the best places to budget-shop; some of the items can be as expensive as those at your local designer boutique.

Top Consignment Shops

Here are some of the best consignment stores across the country. Many of them sell items via the Web. Contact the stores directly for more information.

Nationwide	Buffalo Exchange (www.buffaloexchange.com). National consignment shop with stores in Arizona, California, Colorado, Nevada, New Mexico, Oregon, Pennsylvania, Seattle, Texas, and Wyoming.
Boston	Garment District (www.garmentdistrict.com). Boston's best selection of vintage and thrift items.
Florida	The Snob (www.thesnob.biz). Great selection of St. John Knits.

Los Angeles	Decades Two (www.decadestwo.com). Top celebrity stylists shop at this store.
Los Angeles	Rodeo Drive Resale (www.rodeodriveresale.com). Large selection of high-end designer goods worn by celebs like Reba McEntire.
Massachusetts	Cape Cancer Thrift. Great high-quality vintage accessories.
Minneapolis	Fashion Avenue. Find gently used Chanel tote purses for less than $500.
New York	Ina (www.inanyc.com). This popular consignment shop hosted the *Sex and the City* wardrobe sale.
Philadelphia	Greene Street Consignment (www.greenestreetconsignment.com). An affordable consignment shop. Clothes tend to be from mid-range designers like Anne Klein.

For a more complete listing of consignment shops, visit the National Association of Resale and Thrift Shops (www.narts.org), a twenty-year-old organization that has a searchable database of consignment shops nationwide; the Resale Network (www.resale.net), or TheBudgetFashionista.com. Also check your yellow pages under boutiques or consignment/resale/thrift shops.

Chapter 16

Shopping Online: The Ultimate Budget Shopper's Resource

I have really big feet, and finding stylish shoes in a size 11 used to be a near impossible feat. There were no DSW Shoe Warehouses near me. I was pretty much at the mercy of Nordstrom until I learned the power of shopping online. Increased transaction security and liberal return policies have made shopping online not only easier but also sometimes cheaper than shopping in brick-and-mortar stores.

Online shopping is not only a great resource for budget fashionistas with specific shopping issues but also for those who live outside big cities. Online shopping has leveled the fashion playing field by making your favorite designers available regardless of where you live. Sites like Bluefly.com and Smartbargains.com offer major discounts on such top designers as Prada, Marc Jacobs, Etro, Nanette Lepore, Tracy Reese, and more. All you need is a computer and an Internet hookup.

Online stores are also great places to comparison-shop for designer items. For example, I was looking for a pair of gold sandals from the company Earth. I checked out the price of the shoes at Nordstrom but also looked up the price on the company's website and on Zappos.com. Zappos had the best deal and also offered free shipping and returns.

The Budget Fashionista Explains: How to Shop Online

1. **Check shipping before you buy.** Make sure you check the cost of shipping before you buy. Some online stores make additional money by charging high shipping and packaging charges. Shop at stores that don't offer free or reduced shipping when you're looking for a specific item that can only be found at that store.
2. **Buy what you know.** Experimenting with new products or styles can be costly when shopping online because many sites will make you pay for returning the item.
3. **Check the return policy.** Make sure you've read the store's return policy. Don't buy from a store that doesn't have a return policy.
4. **Look for coupons.** For instance, you can head to TheBudget-Fashionista.com for coupons for your favorite stores.

Best Online Shops

Asos.com (www.asos.com). The British version of Forever 21, this store arranges its selections by the designers and celebrities who influenced the particular item. The site does ship to the United States.

Bluefly (www.bluefly.com). This shop carries top designers—from Prada to Dior to Marc Jacobs—for up to 80 percent off retail prices. Sizes and selections change quickly, so head to the site when you are prepared to buy. They also carry high-end housewares from companies like Frette.

Coco & Delilah (www.coco-delilah.com). Ever hip, this site is great for casual wear from designers such as Tocca, Nanette Lepore, and Lacoste at up to 60 percent off retail prices.

eBay (www.ebay.com). This is a Budget Fashionista's secret weapon. The online auction site is the best place to find designer goods at rock-bottom prices. However, beware of auctions on high-end items that sound too good to be true. Protect yourself by paying for your items with a credit card that has buyer protection or through the eBay-owned Paypal (www.paypal.com) system.

eluxury (www.eluxury.com). Owned by the parent company of Louis Vuitton, this site is the official Louis Vuitton online store and also sells bags from such designers as Celine, Marc Jacobs, and Christian Dior.

La Redoute (www.laredoute.com). French women have been raving for years about La Redoute, and American women can finally benefit from the store's amazing collection as well. The site has special lines from high-end French designers including Jean Paul Gaultier and Cacharel. This store is probably the only place to find a Jean Paul Gaultier bustier for $29.95.

Loehmann's@smartbargains.com (www.smartbargains.com). The online discount shop Smartbargains.com joined forces with offline shopping guru Loehmann's to put the store, including its famous back room, online. All the major players are there including Roberto Cavalli, Givenchy, Anna Sui, and Michael Kors. The site also has an impressive selection of designer sunglasses from Gucci and Chloe for up to 70 percent off the retail price.

Nordstrom (www.nordstrom.com). The online version of this higher-end department store has a large selection of shoes and a decent clearance section. The site is especially good for budget fashionistas with hard-to-find shoe sizes (below a size 6 and above a 10). Particularly impressive is their selection of petite- and plus-size fashions, which is much more diverse and stylish than their in-store offerings.

Overstock (www.overstock.com). The biggest outlet store on the Web, it sells everything from scooters to scarves. It is the perfect one-stop shop for busy moms who want to pick up something for the kids and want to score a little something for their closets. Overstock has its own line of clothing, called Prague, that produces "designer-inspired" fashions.

Yoox (www.yoox.com). This European site is chock-full of the best designers from Gaultier to Galliano. It's sort of like a cool, techno-pop cousin from Italy. You can see what the clothing looks like on the mannequin that floats strangely in the middle of the screen. Selections move fast, so be prepared to purchase what you like because it might not be there when you come back.

Zappos (www.zappos.com). Zappos lives up to its name as the biggest shoe store on the Web, carrying designer shoes and accessories from Vera Wang, Casadei, Judith Leiber, Roberto Cavalli, and more. They have a huge selection and carry tons of sizes. Plus, they always have free shipping.

Budget Fashionista Tip #31: Alternative Outfitters

If you're a vegan/cruelty-free budget fashionista, stores such as Alternative Outfitters (www.alternativeoutfitters.com), Earth (www.earth.us), MooShoes (www.mooshoes.com), and Coquette Faux Furriers (www.coquettefauxfurriers.com) offer fashion-forward, budget friendly, cruelty-free products that won't have you looking as if you just stepped out of a commune. The clothes and accessories at these stores are so stylish and inexpensive that even fur-coat-wearing (from the Salvation Army, of course), fashion-centered budget fashionistas like myself are frequent shoppers. Items like a pair of vegan espadrilles at Alternative Outfitters remind me of a similar pair by Marc Jacobs—just $200 cheaper. The stole collection at Coquette Faux Furriers, inspired by 1950s bombshell icons like Marilyn Monroe, is glamorous and sexy, and allows me to fulfill my dreams of being a Hollywood starlet while being socially conscious. My Gidget boots from the folks at Earth resemble a pair I saw at the hip boutique Scoop NYC.

Alternative fashions are also great options for those who want the fur look on a cotton budget. Faux leather shoes cost up to 75 percent less than similar leather products. Full-length faux fur coats from retailers like Fabulous Furs (www.fabulousfurs.com), retail for up to 65 percent less than comparable real fur coats.

eBay: A Budget Shopper's Dream

The woman who created eBay must have been a budget fashionista at heart. Who else could have come up with the brilliant idea of putting a global garage sale on the Web? The online auction site is a secret shopping destination for millions of fashionistas who want to score fabulous designer products at ultra-low prices. It is particularly helpful for fashion lovers who live outside major cities.

These are some of my top eBay finds:

- pair of mid-calf Ugg boots for $19.99
- vintage black evening dress for $5.99
- pair of Kate Spade slides for $25
- pair of brand-new Frye boots for $40
- vintage Lanvin gray wool pinstriped skirt for $6.99

Shoppers are lured to eBay with promises of finding designer items for much less, but as the old saying goes, you don't get something for nothing. A lot of the new "designer" items on eBay are fake. There are some exceptions to the rule, of course, but for the most part the open market aspect of the auction site (anyone can sell, anyone can buy) makes it easy for anyone—legitimate or not—to sell a product.

To circumvent this issue, I usually focus on purchasing designer items that have been slightly used but are in great shape. This lets me know that the seller has actually used the item and that the price is lower because the product is not brand-new. I always ask for additional pictures of the item, especially if it costs more than $15.

Although I'm a big fan of auction sites like eBay and Yahoo! Auctions, I must advise you to be careful when shopping on the sites. Use your shopping sixth sense, a credit card with buyer protection or a Paypal account, and the earlier tips in this chapter to improve your shopping experience on the site. Never send a money order or cashier's check to a seller because you have little or no recourse if the seller doesn't send you the item or if the item isn't as advertised.

Vintage Shopping Online

EBay isn't the only place to find excellent vintage fashions online. Check out these online stores for high-quality vintage fashions.

Inside Scoop: *Constance White, Personal Style Editor at eBay.com and General Fashion Diva*

Constance White, personal style editor at eBay.com, makes shopping for great fashion deals on eBay easier. A former correspondent for *Full Frontal Fashion* and former editor at *Elle* magazine, she teaches budget fashionistas how to protect themselves on eBay with the following four tips.

1. **Review the seller's feedback.** Feedback is an integral tool on eBay. It helps you see what other eBayers have said about their transactions with the seller and whether they were happy or unhappy. If a seller has positive feedback, then you know you can consider purchasing an item from this person.
2. **Research the price of the item you are considering buying.** You can get good deals on eBay, but you also have to be realistic about the good deals you get. If the price of an item is too good to be true, then walk away from it.
3. **Contact the seller with questions.** Get all your questions answered before you decide to buy an item. If you are still unsure about the item or have lingering questions, don't buy it.
4. **Use a secure payment.** Services like Paypal will further protect your purchase. Both eBay and Paypal offer seller and buyer protection.

Fashion Dig (www.fashiondig.com). The grandma of online vintage sites features a huge database of online and offline vintage stores.

Fever Vintage (www.fevervintage.com). From sequins to polyester pantsuits reminiscent of *Saturday Night Fever*, Fever Vintage sells a large selection of premium fashions for less than $50. The store also has a nice vintage selection for men.

Vintage Trends (www.vintagetrends.com). This large site for men, women, and children offers not only clothing but also military items, lingerie, and housewares. My favorite section is the vintage ethnic clothing from faraway places like Pakistan, Ghana, and Bali. Most items are priced between $20 and $50.

Hey Viv (www.heyviv.com). Looking for clothing and accessories inspired by the 1950s? Dreaming of an outfit that would turn June Cleaver green with envy? This is a great place to look for a poodle skirt. Most items are priced below $40.

The Do-It-Yourself Movement: Not Your Grandma's Knitting Circle

Even with options like eBay, it can be hard to find unique, original clothing on a budget in the mega mall world of mass-produced fashion. One of the best ways to add some originality to your wardrobe is to either make a garment yourself or purchase one from a DIY site. Even if you can't tell your purl from your loop, you can create your own unique fashions and accessories.

Here's a very simple but fun project to get your DIY juices flowing. You'll need the following items:

- glue gun
- package of sequins
- ruler
- tailor's chalk
- garment (shirt, skirt, pants, etc.)

This project is a great way to spruce up a plain top, skirt, or pants. If this is your first time using a glue gun, choose an old shirt or top. A glue gun in the wrong hands could mean serious problems. Go to your nearest craft store and purchase the coolest package of sequins or jewel-like embellishments you can find (more if you want a Liberace-like effect).

Take the garment and lay it flat on a table; a kitchen table works well. Use the ruler and tailor's chalk to mark out a pattern for the sequins. Heat up the glue gun and put the glue on the sequins, not the garment. Place the sequins on the garment and let dry about thirty minutes. The result will be a truly original item of clothing.

Inside Scoop: *Leah Kramer, Founder of Craftster.org*

Leah Kramer is one crafty chick. As the queen bee of crafty, Leah is the founder of the forty thousand-plus-member craft social network, Craftster.org. She is also the organizer of Bazaar Bizarre, a popular Boston craft fair. A self-professed craft junky, she was that kid at summer camp who would spend the whole time making all her cabinmates fabulous friendship bracelets. Leah gives us some tips on how to uncover our inner craftsters, and she shares recipes for two simple yet fashionable craft projects that we can do ourselves.

Why should budget fashionistas buy from a DIY site?

When you buy from a DIY site, you're far more likely to get something truly unique. You won't see your next-door neighbor wearing the same garment. You are also supporting an emerging designer or artist and small-business person.

What are some of your favorite DIY sites?

One of my favorites is Boy Girl Party (www.boygirlparty.com). The woman behind it is both a talented crafter and an amazing illustrator and artist. She integrates her art into her crafts in really appealing ways. I also love My Paper Crane (www.mypapercrane.com). The crafter behind this site makes these unique plush toys and cute little paintings that have a style unlike anything I've ever seen.

I know that as the headmistress of crafty, you have the recipes to some great DIY projects. Please share one or two very simple projects with us.

Here are two that you might enjoy.

Fake Flower Accessory—requires the following materials:

- fake flower
- blank pin or blank barrette
- hot-glue gun

This fun project involves finding a cool fake flower and then hot-gluing it onto a pin to create a flower pin. Craft stores often have huge selections of fake flowers, so you're sure to find some styles that appeal to you. I've also found fashionable fake flowers at dollar stores. Just cut off the stem of the fake flower, put some hot glue on the base of the flower, and press it against the base of a blank pin. Blank pins can be found at craft stores in the jewelry supply section, or you can just push a large safety pin through the back of the flower. You can also glue the flower onto a plain barrette for a quick hair accessory.

Ribbon Headband—requires these materials:

- 16 inches of ribbon
- 5 inches of ¼-inch-wide sewing elastic
- antifray solution
- needle and thread

I love to make headbands out of cool ribbons. You can use preppy striped ribbon, floral, leopard print . . . whatever you like! To make a ribbon headband, dab some antifray solution onto the ends of the ribbon so it doesn't fray. You can find this solution at a sewing store or in the glue section of a craft store. Wait for the solution to dry. Then with a needle and thread sew one end of the elastic to the "wrong side" of one end of the ribbon and sew the other end of the elastic to the wrong side of the other end.

Some Great DIY Sites

On TheBudgetFashionista.com I try to be as supportive of up-and-coming do-it-yourself designers as I am of the big design houses. Run by industrious and talented designers, DIY stores are great places for budget fashionistas to find high-quality one-of-a-kind items.

Crafty Ass Chick (www.craftyasschick.com). This is one of the best-designed craft sites on the Web. With items ranging from stationery to hand-spun yarn, this Crafty Ass Chick definitely lives up to her name.

Trashy Magazine (www.trashymagazine.com). I love everything about this little online thrift store and magazine—from the cool brown and white polka-dot motif to the hip T-shirts and jewelry sold for below $20. Many of the items displayed were revamped or restyled by the shop's owner and webmaster, Crystal.

Lekkner (www.lekkner.com). This DIY site has some of the cutest handmade items on the net. Find cute accessories such as a bag made of old men's ties and a vintage NFL handbag.

Belle Style (www.bellestyle.com). Inspired by the likes of Matisse and Van Gogh, the designers behind Belle Style make incredible stone jewelry. Skip the intro (the swirling flash makes me dizzy) and head right to the merchandise. I can't wait for the Frida Kahlo line.

Primp Shop (www.primpshop.com). I'm in love with Primp Shop's crocheted flower pins.

Whether it's shopping on eBay or supporting an up-and-coming DIY designer, shopping on the Web is a great resource for budget shoppers. In the next chapter, you'll see how to use the tips and tricks learned in this and previous chapters in real-life situations.

Chapter 17

Putting It All Together

Below are several real-life budget fashion questions posed on my website by fashionistas like yourself. These questions and their answers demonstrate how to use the principles learned in this book.

Shopping Case Study #1: First Job Interview

Dear Budget Fashionista:

I'm a senior in college, and I'm preparing for my first professional job interviews. All I have in my closet are a few pairs of jeans and a couple of those shirts I got for signing up for credit cards. I need interview clothes.

Help!

Need a Job in Denver, Colorado

Dear Need a Job:

College students never have money. It is inherent in the nature of higher education. However, you need to look as professional as possible for your first job interviews. The following are just a couple of ways that you can obtain a basic interview suit with little or no money.

1. **Friend or relative.** If you're really broke, borrow something. It is the easiest and the cheapest way to get an outfit quickly. And unlike an outfit from Goodwill, you know where it has been.
2. **Thrift stores.** These stores have tons of suits from Jones New York to Tahari to some cheaper generic brands. You will be able to find a suit for well under $20.
3. **Off-price stores like Marshalls, T.J. Maxx, and Ross.** Easy and accessible, these stores always have basics like black suits.
4. **Outlets.** The outlets of such designers as Tahari, Anne Klein, and Jones New York are all great places to look for an inexpensive basic black suit.
5. **Department stores.** Lord & Taylor, Macy's, Profitt, and Marshall Field's have a large selection of black and blue business suits at very reasonable prices.

The interview suit should be a plain black or navy blue suit. Even if you are applying for a job in a more creative field, start off with a basic suit. Leave the low-rise jeans and thong sandals at home. Wait until you're hired to demonstrate your personality in your clothing.

Happy Shopping,

The Budget Fashionista

Shopping Case Study #2: *Rising Up the Corporate Ladder*

Dear Budget Fashionista:

I'm a thirty-two-year-old middle manager at a very prestigious insurance company in the Midwest. I'm desperately trying to make my way up the corporate ladder, but with my massive student loans, I can barely afford to pay my mortgage let alone purchase a whole new wardrobe. How can I look like a corporate climber without tapping into my 401(k)?

Yours in fashion,

Corporate Climber in Chaska, Minnesota

Dear Corporate Climber:

You don't have to give up your fashion identity just because you work in a sea of grays and blues. Believe it or not, there are a couple of things you can do with your corporate blues to maintain both a sense of style and your 401(k). We'll get you to the corner office in no time.

Remember the old saying: "You must look like money in order to make money." Use your signature piece to maintain your fashion identity and convey your position as a corporate mover and shaker. Try signature pieces that easily display status: examples are an expensive Michelle watch, a Montblanc pen, or a Tods satchel with matching accessories. Stores such as Off 5th, Saks Fifth Avenue Outlet and Last Call Neiman Marcus; the outlets of major designers such as Burberry, Ellen Tracy, and Armani; and online stores like Ashford.com and Yoox.com are great places to look for these items at a fraction of their original cost.

In order to get the most mileage out of these accessories, always show up at office meetings slightly later than everyone else (but on time, of course). Always remove your jacket or wear short-sleeved shirts to show off your fancy watch or carefully tap your Montblanc pen to your chin during meetings so that everyone can see your status symbol.

Since suits are a staple of your daily work wardrobe, choose suits with more of a feminine cut from designers like Theory and Anne Klein (found at most department stores). Look for suits with visible but not overbearing patterns, such as a blue pin-striped suit or a herringbone tweed suit. Although tailored suits would be the ultimate suiting for you, they can be pricey, so get the next best thing: Purchase your suits and then have them tailored to a perfect fit. Most major department stores offer tailoring services, or you can try your local dry cleaner. You could also wear a sexy but supportive bra and panty set under your drab work clothes. You might do like one Budget Fashionista reader and purchase a Wonder Woman lingerie set to wear underneath your suit to give you a boost of confidence.

To transition your suit from day to night, purchase a pair of sexy three-inch strappy designer sandals from a store like DSW Shoe Warehouse and one of the Mossimo silk camisoles from Target. Add to the mix a pair of colorful chandelier or gold hoop earrings.

Happy Shopping,

The Budget Fashionista

Shopping Case Study #3: *Postpartum Fashion Predicament*

Dear Budget Fashionista:

I recently had a beautiful baby. I used to be a size 10, but now I am a size 14, with most of my weight in the midsection. What essentials should I buy to wear back to work this fall? I want some mix-and-match pieces at good prices. I don't want to spend too much money since I don't plan to hang out in this size too long.

I need assistance!

Fashionable Mommy in Dallas, Texas

Dear Fashionable Mommy:

Congrats on the baby. One of the hardest things to do, fashion wise, is make the transition from stay-at-home mom to working mama. In order to get you ready for your return to work, purchase the following items:

- A good black pantsuit with a tailored jacket that hits slightly below your bottom. It should be made of either a light wool (gabardine) material or a light rayon-wool blend.
- Tailored collared cotton shirts and sweaters in white, black, and a color such as pink or purple. Try the Isaac Mizrahi line at Target. Make sure you wash sweaters in cold water and dry them flat to retain their shape.
- One pair of fitted boot-cut jeans that hit slightly below the waist (avoid an extremely low rise). Old Navy and Gap have an amazing selection of jeans and corduroys for well under $30. Look for a spandex content of 2 to 5 percent to help hold in the problem spots.
- An A-line skirt in black and gray that hits slightly mid-calf. Pair it up with a cute pair of knee-high boots with a small heel.
- Accessories. Stock up on these, since you can use them no matter what your size. Lord & Taylor, Macy's, Marshall Field's, and Kohl's all have great jewelry at reasonable prices. Use necklaces, earrings, and bracelets to add spice to otherwise boring outfits.
- A bra and underwear. Run to your nearest intimates section and get fitted for a bra. After having a baby, you are probably not the same bra

size. Also look for underwear with a little spandex to help pull in problem areas.

Using items from your Perfect Ten (see page 65) and the above purchases, you can create outfit combinations such as:

- khakis, cotton sweater, and flats
- A-line skirt, white collared shirt, black boots, and pearl necklace
- khakis, white collared shirt, black boots, black blazer (from black suit), and brooch
- black pants (from black suit), cotton sweater, black heels, and pearl necklace
- A-line skirt, cotton sweater, blazer, and black heels

Happy Shopping!

The Budget Fashionista

Shopping Case Study #4:

Confronting the Past: The High School Reunion

Dear Budget Fashionista:

My ten-year high school reunion is coming up, and I want to look fabulous. There are two events: the Happy Hour and the Reunion Dinner Party. How can I wow my old classmates without breaking the bank?

Help!

Best Dressed in Sacramento, California

Dear Best Dressed:

Follow these steps to wow your former classmates:

For the happy hour you want to be casual but stylish. Wear a nice pair of fitted jeans with a slight boot-cut. Buy a fitted blazer in a trendy fabric that hits you right at your waist. Purchase or borrow a brooch from your grandmother and pair it up with a pair of fake diamond earrings that look at least one carat. Constantly place your hair behind your ears all night long so everyone can get a good look at the earrings. Wear a pair of sexy black pumps and bring a nice little black clutch.

For the reunion dinner party you want to look dressy but not too dressy. Start off with a very simple classic little black dress. The dress needs to fit perfectly to carry off this look, so head to your nearest tailor if necessary. Wear any color shoe you can find *except* black, and they must be pumps at least three inches high. Think red, orange, silver, etc. Pumps elongate your legs, making you appear thinner and more statuesque. Zappos.com has the best selection of sexy pumps. Buy a purse that complements the shoes and resist the urge to wear black nylons.

The most important thing to wear is a smile. At least you don't have to take gym class again.

Happy Shopping,

The Budget Fashionista

Shopping Case Study #5: *Career Changer*

Dear Budget Fashionista:

For twelve years I was in corporate America where I was required to have a conservative wardrobe. I now own an event-planning company that services the entertainment industry. How can I transition my "rigid" corporate wardrobe to something that fits both the new role and me without breaking the bank?

Thanks,

Career Changer in Raleigh, North Carolina

Dear Career Changer:

It truly takes guts to go out on your own. However, don't throw your black, blue, and gray suits out with your key card. You can even hold on to those "sensible" black pumps. Use these pieces as the foundation for your new wardrobe and then add the following pieces to update your wardrobe to reflect your current position.

- Two pairs of comfortable strappy heels, one in black and one in some outrageous color like hot pink.
- Shoe jewelry (like the old school shoe buckles your grandma used to

wear). You can find great shoe jewelry at Nordstrom or at Baker's Shoes. You are going to put this jewelry on your old "sensible" shoes. As an event planner you will be running around quite a bit, so you'll still need to be comfortable.

- Three slip tops: one sequined, one camisole, and another with a slight shimmer. These tops should fit very well and should be any color but black.
- As many earrings, necklaces, and bracelets as you can get your hands on. You will use these to accessorize your current outfits.
- Two nice party dresses in any color but black.
- One tailored blazer in any color but black.
- A nice cashmere sweater set. It's classic and can go with everything. Score a sweater for well under $60 from Macy's or Smartbargains.com.

The above items can help you easily transform your wardrobe from corporate drag to perfect planner. As an event planner you must be stylish, and the above items will mix well with your corporate pieces. For evening events take that black suit and pair it up with a colorful sequined top and a pair of strappy heels. For events during the day, wear either a pair of pants or a skirt from one of your nonblack suits with your cashmere twin set. Again, throw on a necklace or brooch, some simple pearl earrings, and a pair of your sensible shoes (don't forget the shoe jewelry), and you will be ready to go. Now go forth and plan!

Happy Shopping,

The Budget Fashionista

Shopping Case Study #6: *Stylish at Sixty*

Dear Budget Fashionista:

I'm a style-conscious sixty-seven-year-old from Miami. I find it difficult to know what to wear without looking matronly. How can I build a stylish wardrobe without looking like a clown?

Please help!

Rockin' Grandma in Miami, Florida

Dear Rockin' Grandma:

Who says you can't be sassy at sixty? Granted, a spandex miniskirt may not be on your fashion horizon at the moment, but there are many other fashion options for the "mature" woman. Led by Susan Sarandon, Barbara Walters, and Lee Radziwill, sixty is now the new forty.

The first step is for you to remove the following from your closet ASAP:

- large print floral dresses
- muumuus (unless they are for lounging around the house)
- long (ankle-length) unstructured skirts, especially those made of denim or chambray
- full elastic waist pants that make everyone look like a balloon
- those hideous unlined, unstructured pantsuits in polyester or linen in unflattering pastel colors
- unstylish jumper-type dresses (usually made of khaki or jean material)

Embrace the following:

- **Monochrome.** Wear one simple color (black, white, khaki, etc.) from head to toe. This will create a slimming effect and is a classic look for any age.
- **Jewelry for color.** Fashionistas pay big bucks for pieces you already have in your jewelry box. Wear your beaded necklaces, bracelets, and other jewelry from your youth to add color to your outfits.
- **Boot-cut pants.** Buy a pair of tailored boot-cut pants in black, white, or khaki in light fabrics like cotton and rayon. Not only will you be comfortable, but this will also draw attention away from your midsection and give you a slightly taller look, which is important as you get older. Look for pants with a little spandex/Lycra content, which will help control any problem areas. For skirts, stick to straight cuts that hit mid-calf.
- **The mid-heel.** Pair the boot-cut pants with sandals that have a small heel. The shoe company Clarks (www.clarks.com) carries hot sandals that are both comfortable and extremely stylish. The comfort giant Naturalizer now carries a line of sandals from über-trendy designer Tara Subkoff.

- **Fitted T-shirts.** Throw in a couple of fitted (not tight) T-shirts and tanks to wear underneath lightweight, slightly big cotton sweaters or cotton blazers.
- **A subscription to *Harper's Bazaar*.** This venerable fashion magazine features styles for women of all ages.

Here are some sample outfits you can make from the above items:

- white T-shirt, white cotton boot-cut pants, and black, navy blue, or red jacket
- white cotton sweater, black pants, and cute sandals
- black T-shirt, black pants, and funky jewelry

Check out these designers:

St. John Knits: pricey, but the knit pieces can be worn year-round

Eileen Fisher: long, flowing garments made of a variety of lightweight cottons and rayons

Liz Claiborne: perfect for Florida weather and extremely comfortable

Ralph Lauren: Comfortable, classic, casual pieces that can be found on sale at T.J. Maxx, Marshalls, or your local department store

The Gap: Not just for kids, this is the best place to buy reasonably priced jeans and khakis regardless of age and also great basic T-shirts

Old Navy: basic T-shirts and jeans at reasonable prices

Happy Shopping,

The Budget Fashionista

Congratulations— You've Made It!

You're now a budget fashionista. You understand your style, you have your stores, you know how to take care of your clothes to prolong usage, and you faithfully put money into your shopping savings account every month.

But before I send you off to the budget-shopping trenches, don't forget these words of wisdom:

- **Never buy something just because it's on sale.** It's a waste, not a bargain, if you never wear the piece.
- **Always buy the best-quality items you can get on sale.** If they wear out so quickly that you have to replace them often, then you're really not getting a deal.
- **Fit is more important than size.** Different designers use different fit models, affecting the cut of the garment. Always try on a size smaller and a size bigger to get the right fit.
- **Focus on purchasing complete outfits,** which will save you a great deal of time in the morning when you need to dress quickly.
- **Try EVERYTHING on, regardless of the price.** Many stores now have strict return policies. Plus, you'll save yourself a trip.
- **Always wear good undergarments when shopping.** This will affect how a piece of clothing looks on your body.
- **LOVE what you BUY and only BUY what you LOVE.**

This book is only the beginning. I have a whole slew of (free!) tools, tips, and guides available to support you on your mission to look fabulous for less. Visit TheBudgetFashionista.com for guides, tools, and tips to help you dress and look your best. Feel free to e-mail me at kathrynbook@thebudgetfashionista.com with any questions or comments. Sign up for our newsletters and get the scoop on the latest shopping tips, best coupons, and hottest fashion trends.

Become a Certified Budget Fashionista!

Visit my website (www.thebudgetfashionista.com) and enter the password htbbfbook2006 to take your quiz and receive your budget fashionista certificate, certifying you as a true budget fashionista. This certificate will allow you to obtain additional coupons and deals from selected retailers.

As I stated at the beginning, my purpose in writing this book was to increase the number of active, as opposed to passive, consumers who understand that looking great doesn't have to mean financial ruin. Despite what the media and advertisers may say, you have the power to look great regardless of your size, economic status, or geographical location. I hope this book has helped you on this path.

Appendix A: TheBudgetFashionista.com Online Budget Resources

GENERAL FINANCIAL INFO

Kiplinger (www.kiplinger.com). Kiplinger has been a trusted source for personal financial advice for over eighty years. Their financial tutorials give you the scoop on everything from how to get the best mortgage to how to build a stock portfolio.

The Beehive (www.beehive.org). This nonprofit website has great tips for good health, jobs, and family. They have one of the best and easiest to use online budget calculators.

Money/CNN (www.money.com). *Money* magazine teamed up with CNN to offer detailed financial calculators on the Web. You can calculate everything from your estimated monthly mortgage to your total debt.

Morningstar (www.morningstar.com). Financial planners use this site religiously. Morningstar has up-to-date information on mutual funds and historic stock performance.

FINANCIAL ADVICE

Here are some great places to check out financial information:

The Motley Fool (www.fool.com). Realistic financial advice for even the most "foolish" fashionista.

Consumer Credit Counseling Service (CCCS) (www.nfcc.org). This nonprofit agency can help you figure out how to control and manage your debt effectively. It also offers debt reduction plans.

Suze Orman (www.suzeorman.com). This financial guru gives straightforward, easy-to-implement advice on a whole slew of financial issues.

Fannie Mae (www.fanniemae.org). This is a great site for those looking for guidance on everything from managing finances to purchasing a house.

Credit Scores

There are three main credit reporting agencies: Experian, Equifax, and Trans Union. Make sure you check all three for your credit ratings.

Experian: www.experian.com
Equifax: www.equifax.com
Trans Union: www.transunion.com

Online Debt Calculators

www.money.com
www.smartmoney.com
www.bankone.com

Appendix B: The Budget Fashionista's Mini-Guide to Taking Care of Clothes

THE BUDGET FASHIONISTA'S KEY LAUNDRY TIPS

- Turn clothes inside out to protect color and extend the life of the garment.
- Read the care labels carefully and follow them.
- Always check pockets for lipstick, pens, and other items.
- Use liquid baby detergent rather than Woolite to wash your delicates because it is much cheaper and gentler.
- Add one-half cup of baking soda to the wash to act as a fabric softener.
- Use the following guide to help sort laundry according to colors and fabrics:

Water	Temperature Fahrenheit/Celsius	Clothing
Hot	130/54	Whites, colorfast, heavily soiled
Warm	100/37	Non-colorfast, permanent press, knits, woolens, silk
Cold	80/26	Dark colors that fade, bright colors, non-colorfast

HOW TO REMOVE STAINS

Accidents do happen, but that's not a reason to throw out your favorite top. Save your stained garments from the Goodwill bin by using the guide below to quickly and effectively remove stains.

Stain	Remedy	Instructions
Baby spit-up	Powder detergent	Apply to a wet garment, leave it on for a while, and then rinse off.
Beer	Cold water and white vinegar	Soak in 2 cups cold water and ½ cup white vinegar for approximately 5 minutes.
Blood	Baking soda and water	Make a paste, apply it, let sit for a few minutes, then rinse with cold water.
Chocolate, red wine	Club soda, mild detergent (such as Ivory dishwashing liquid), and cold water	Rinse with club soda, apply detergent, then rinse with cold water.
Coffee, cigarettes	Hand soap	Apply and then rinse with cold water
Gum	Home freezer	The gum will get hard in freezer, and you will be able to scrape it off.
Lipstick, makeup, ink, highlighter	Cheap aerosol hair spray	Spray on stain, let sit for a few minutes, then rinse with cold water.
Self-tanning lotion	Hydrogen peroxide	Dab on using a cotton ball.
White wine	White vinegar	Apply a small amount and then rinse with cold water.

Acknowledgments

First and foremost I would like to thank every budget fashionista who ever visited the site, sent me an e-mail, or bought this book. We are living proof that you don't have to be a millionaire to look fabulous. I would also like to thank the William D. Ford Federal Direct Loan Program for giving me thirty years to pay back my student loans.

Warm fuzzies to the folks at Random House/Ballantine books, especially my editor, Christina Duffy, who has yet to recover from hanging out with me during Fashion Week. Big ups to my literary agent, Nicholas Lewis, for believing in the power of TBF, and to Aimee Sicuro and Tobias Wright for enhancing TheBudgetFashionista.com (and this book) with their illustrations. Many thanks to Debby Fowler, Kevin Matthews, Janine Moore, Leah Kramer, Elke Von Freudenberg, Elissa Bloom, David Wolfe, Cate Cochran, Lynne Mastrilli, and Constance White for letting me pick their brains and for adding their advice to this book. Homage to assistants, both past and present, Rebecca, Harsimran, and Jennifer, and a very special thanks to Mel B.

My family has been participants, willing and very often unwilling, in my escapades. Thanks to my mom, Karen, and to my late father, Robert, for always being my biggest fans. Thanks to my grandma Doonie for inspiring me, and special thanks to my brother, Rob, for forgiving me when I "borrowed" his clothes in junior high. A special thanks to all of my family and friends.

And to Tobias, thanks for loving me enough to let me turn you into a Budget Manista.